C000109257

LEARIE

THE MAN WHO BROKE THE COLOUR BAR

LEARIE

THE MAN WHO BROKE THE COLOUR BAR

BRIAN SCOVELL

The Book Guild Ltd

First published in Great Britain in 2021 by
The Book Guild Ltd
9 Priory Business Park
Wistow Road, Kibworth
Leicestershire, LE8 0RX
Freephone: 0800 999 2982
www.bookguild.co.uk
Email: info@bookguild.co.uk
Twitter: @bookguild

Copyright © 2021 Brian Scovell

The right of Brian Scovell to be identified as the author of this
work has been asserted by him in accordance with the
Copyright, Design and Patents Act 1988.

All rights reserved. No part of this publication may be
reproduced, transmitted, or stored in a retrieval system, in any form or by any means,
without permission in writing from the publisher, nor be otherwise circulated in
any form of binding or cover other than that in which it is published and without
a similar condition being imposed on the subsequent purchaser.

Typeset in 11pt Minion Pro

Printed and bound by CPI Group (UK) Ltd, Croydon, CR0 4YY

ISBN 978 1913551 483

British Library Cataloguing in Publication Data.
A catalogue record for this book is available from the British Library.

MIX
Paper from
responsible sources
FSC® C013604

Acknowledgements

A host of good people helped me to write the story of this remarkable, decent man Learie Constantine. First Solly Chandler, the sports editor of the now defunct Daily Sketch in early 1963. He wasn't a cricket fan and probably he hadn't heard of Learie but he knew the sports writer Reg Hayter, who launched a sport agency with his name. Reg ghost wrote Denis Compton's columns in 1947 when the Middlesex player scored 3,816 runs and eighteen centuries, records that have never been bettered. He was inundated with letters and asked Reg if could he take charge of it. The absent minded Compton (1918-1997) was my first cricketing hero and got to know him well when I started writing for the Daily Sketch.

Reg knew Bagenal Harvey, one of the first sporting agents, and recommended him to sign up Compton. The exotically named Bagenal was named after the United Irish Republican commander Beauchamp Bagenal Havey who led the Irish against the British Army in 1798 in the battle of New Ross. Bagenal had lots of critics because cricket lovers thought agents were dodgy people and some newspapers labelled him 'Mr X' including the Sketch.

Reg introduced him to Learie who had just resigned as the first High Commissioner of Trinidad and Tobago in Britain and needed extra income to complete his training as a barrister. If Compton hadn't become famous through the selling expertise of Bagenal Learie wouldn't have become the Daily Sketch's first cricket analyst. There were posters all over the country advertising Brylcreem using Compton's picture. Half the male population used Brylcreem for a while.

I got to know all these people and they were fine men.

The next person to be mentioned was my late wife Audrey who soon became friends of Learie and Lady Norma and they became godparents of my daughter Louise in 1967. Audrey's parents were Lucy O'Sullivan, a much loved Welsh lady with nine children and an inventor Irishman Eric O'Sullivan. The children grew up in India and they made an early start to understand diversity.

After Learie sadly died at the age of sixty nine in 1971, and soon Norma died in the following year, we went to see their only child, the Hon Gloria Valere and his lawyer husband Andre. They were lovely, talented people and their son Maurice, a lawyer and his family were equally impressive. I thank them sincerely for their memories of Learie and Norma.

My final dedication is to my family. When the beautiful Audrey, an etcher of the Royal Academy, died on Christmas Day 2000 I wrote an article in the Daily Mail about my psychic experiences following her departure. Lots of ladies wrote to me and one, Gillian wrote a wonderful, heart warming letter. Her husband John died at the same age as Audrey – 58 – of the same disease, cancer of the liver. Gill has six sisters and Audrey had the same number and her grave grave is 250ms across the road. Gill, a former head mistress, is making our lives happy and contented.

ONE

A TORCH-BEARER FOR THE WEST INDIES

The first aspect one noticed of the Baron Learie Nicholas Constantine of Maraval in Trinidad and Tobago and Nelson in the Palatine of Lancaster was his laugh. He was a truly happy man whose guffaw outdid most people's and a glimpse of his shoulders and his chest heaving was a memorable sight. Once seen, never forgotten.

He had a wonderful sense of humour and on my many visits to Trinidad and most of the Caribbean islands since 1967 I soon realised his humour was a major plus of the Afro-Caribbean people. Learie was descended from slaves in Africa and with many dying en route in inhuman conditions the survivors needed some relief when they landed. And when the exodus to Great Britain after WW2 began they needed to smile and hold their heads high. Learie soon became a torch-bearer for his people, in hard times.

I was lucky enough to spend five summers between 1965–9 as cricket correspondent of the *Daily Sketch* working with him. He took over from Jim Laker, who had a four-year stint; Jim wrote his own copy and, later on, phoned it over to the *Sketch*. Solly Chandler, the sports editor of the *Sketch*, had little knowledge of cricket and his successor, Scotsman Bob Findlay, also from the *Daily Express*, knew marginally more. They relied on the advice of Keith Miller, the great Australian all-rounder, and Bagenal Harvey, the Irishman who acted as agent of Denis Compton. Both thought Learie would shake up the cautious English players whose main aim in life was to qualify for a benefit. He did… but it took fifty years before they got the message, with Andrew Strauss, the now ECB Director, telling them to be more aggressive in 2016.

Findlay signed up Keith 'Nugget' Miller to write a cricketing column when he was sports editor of the *Daily Express* and Keith used to give him horse-racing tips. Most of them proved to be costly mistakes. The flamboyant Miller often arrived at matches after lunch and the other journalists had to supply him the facts about the first two or three hours of play. Before the close of play he had phoned his 400 words and was ready to go off to see a beautiful lady companion, not one, but many. He was a true cricketing Casanova.

Learie wrote six books, mainly about advising young people how to play cricket, and was able to write a good article himself but he recognised that the *Sketch* had an earlier first edition than all the other national newspapers and speed was essential. At tea intervals in Test matches he gave his opinions about the happenings of the day – who was at fault and who was doing a good job. It was trenchant stuff enough, but true and honest.

He was trained in his youth to type at a fast pace and so was I. He was happy to leave the writing of his 500 or so words to me. Half an hour later I would hand the corrected copy to a phonist who dictated the words to a copytaker at Carmelite House off Fleet Street, the headquarters of the *Sketch*, which had one of the best views of the Thames on Victoria Embankment. The dark and dingy *Daily Mail* was hidden away sixty metres back, also owned by Associated Newspapers.

Learie wasn't making a fortune at the time and was grateful for the rather modest amount of money from the *Sketch*. I was his chauffeur as well as his ghost. Earlier in his career he owned cars but living in a high-rise block of flats in Kendall Court on the Edgware Road he dispensed with a car. He was the ideal passenger and the hours spent together before motorways – the 193-mile-long M1 was being built from 1959 to 1968 – were like sitting alongside an eminent university lecturer who specialised in imparting knowledge about the game of cricket. I learned so much from him.

In 1965 there were two Test series. He was happy giving his views about the New Zealanders but declined to be involved in writing about the South Africa team in the second half of the season because of its government's policy of apartheid, separating black people from white. One column ended up saying, 'Sir Learie's South African Tailpiece – Regarding my refusal to report the South African matches, will all those who wrote – friendly, abusive and anonymous pieces – undertake to invite me to South Africa and have me put up in the same hotels as themselves, use transport, with etc? Or is that bringing sport into politics?' A man named Childs, of Poplar Avenue, Bedworth, Warwickshire, had his letter published the following week.

It said, 'A reader of your paper for many years and I was delighted to hear, by the way of TV news, that Sir Learie Constantine would not be covering any more games for the *Sketch*. It came as something of a shock to read however, that, after breaking his contract, he would still be writing for the paper. Maybe you would like to print his carping comments on British cricket but, thank goodness, I am not forced to read any more. Until the football season, goodbye *Daily Sketch*.'

Learie missed a memorable three Test series with Peter Van der Merwe leading the Springboks, as they were called, winning by 1–0. He would have appreciated the skills of the Pollock brothers, with the fiery Peter, later to become a priest, taking 10-87 and Graeme scoring a magnificent 125 in only 118 minutes in the Trent Bridge Test. The average scoring in the series was around 2.25 an over. These days in Test cricket with batsmen, using superior weapons with supercharged bats, it is four an over, or more. The dynamic fielding of Colin Bland might have reminded Learie that his own fielding would have been in the same class. Sir Donald Bradman once called Learie 'the outstanding fielder in his time' and his record of 28 catches in his 18 Tests was remarkable.

His party trick was to speed off to where a high ball was coming down in the field and appeared to have gone too far. Spectators thought he would miss it. But he put his arms behind his back and would catch the ball without looking. No one has copied it. They couldn't: only he could do it.

As the Trent Bridge Test ended we were delayed waiting for interviews after the match. And my colleague Ian Wooldridge, a slow writer and a great one, was still working in the press box three hours afterwards and saw most of the South Africans go out to the middle, unzip their trousers and pee all over the pitch as a strange form of celebration, probably a first in cricket history. Perhaps it meant more: looking down on the English. Learie wouldn't have liked that. The story was a scoop for Wooldridge's *Daily Mail*. Bob Findlay rang me at breakfast next day and reprimanded me for missing it. When I told Learie he chuckled. 'Blame me, we were too quick to leave the ground and go home!' he said. He never stayed for celebratory drinks, often free from the sponsors, after these matches. He was a family man and loved being with them.

In the following year, in 1966, Learie was back in action ready for England's campaign against the West Indies, commenting on the West Indies tour. On one occasion at the Old Trafford Test there was a break for rain and most of the crowd were leaving. Learie and I were going down the rickety sixty-four steps from the wooden press box and at the bottom a man with a boy aged around twelve was holding his autograph book ready for Learie to sign. Learie took it and wrote an encouraging comment in it and then started interviewing the boy. 'Do you play cricket?' he said. This went on for several minutes, despite the rain. 'Who is your cricket hero?' he asked. 'You, sir,' he replied. Learie roared with laughter. 'I haven't played for twenty or more years. People won't have heard of me.' The father interrupted. 'Oh no,' he said. 'You are a household name. Everyone has heard of you.'

A photographer from the *Sketch* had earlier taken a picture of Wes Hall, swishing and missing the ball bowled by the boy in the nets before the game started in the morning and he suggested that a picture be taken of Learie and the lad. It was filed to the *Sketch* photograph department and it appeared in the newspaper next day. 'Another scoop!' said Learie with a laugh.

Rod Bransgrove, the chairman of Hampshire CCC and the man responsible for building the Ageas Bowl, one of the most beautiful Test match grounds in the world, recalled a similar incident. 'When I was a teenage autograph hunter in the mid sixties, my dad pointed out Sir Learie at the Oval. He was just getting into his large limousine (he was the High Commissioner of Trinidad and Tobago in Britain) and when I asked him for his autograph he invited me to sit in the limo. I don't remember what he said and, in truth, I'd never even seen him play but he was a delightful man and happily signed my album before saying goodbye to both myself and my father.'

Learie made a comeback as a player in the following year, after some persuasion by his chauffeur and ghost. During the second half of the year there was a drought and both of us were suffering the effects of hay fever. Someone from Havering

Cricket Club, in Essex, had arranged a benefit match for charity on June 12th and wanted Learie to turn out. He was sixty-five and hadn't played a game for a few years but agreed somewhat reluctantly. I still have the letter from Charlie Tranter, the Hon Secretary, dated July 1st saying, 'Many thanks for your kind letter on the "gen" on your team and I am sure the bar will be open should you wish to clear the Essex dust from your throat when you get here. If you find time, I should be obliged if you would tell Sir Leary (*sic*) that the Club is indeed honoured to have such a distinguished guest to open its new pavilion.' On arrival he was greeted like royalty and an official of the club found a pair of flannels with a forty-four-inch waist and he was relieved that the trousers fitted him. Havering had links with royalty in its early days. Edward the Confessor (1003–1066) was reputed to have stayed at the Palace in the then village.

I signed up Mick Norman, the Northamptonshire batsman, and Jim Standen, the medium swing bowler of Worcestershire, who was the first-choice goalkeeper of West Ham. Lisa, Jim's ebullient wife, took up the spirit of the occasion, as we did as well. Showers interrupted a low-scoring game and our All Stars only managed 115. Learie came in at six cheered by a rain-soaked audience of several hundred and smashed six sixes before being caught for 66. 'Not quite my age!' he laughed as he came in.

The Havering players, amazed by someone of his age striking the ball so far, were struggling until I took Jim off and put on a guest player whose bowling enabled the home side to win by one wicket. Wisely, Learie decided not to bowl and fielded at first slip without touching the ball. On the drive home he dropped off to sleep.

My artist wife Audrey and I were becoming good friends with the Constantines and when Dr James, the family doctor, told Audrey that she was pregnant, she suggested that Learie and Norma might be invited to become the godparents. I rang Learie and put it to him and after consulting Norma, they agreed. They were delighted. Both were devoted Catholics and took their duties seriously when the christening took place on December 3rd, 1967 in the Catholic church in Addiscombe, near where we lived in Davidson Road, Croydon. The author D.H. Lawrence taught at a school a few hundred metres up the road in the 1920s. Our daughter Louise Jayne behaved beautifully and it was a memorable, happy day.

Learie and Norma also attended our wedding at the fifteenth-century Crosby Hall on the north side of Battersea Bridge where Richard III, Henry VIII, Sir Thomas More, Queen Elizabeth I, Sir Francis Drake, Sir Walter Raleigh and William Shakespeare had dined at various times. It was rebuilt in 1675 after it was burned down and in 1908 it was scheduled to be destroyed but heritage devotees intervened. The Great Hall was dismantled and rebuilt, brick by brick, at Cheyne Walk, Chelsea, site of Sir Thomas More's country garden. In the early 1970s a tycoon named Christopher Moran, learning that the GLC had been disbanded by Margaret Thatcher, bought the leasehold and spent £25m renovating it. Audrey contacted their office and asked the price for hiring it for our wedding. It was just £10.

The wedding took place on October 1st, 1965 and the Constantines travelled from their home to Cheyne Walk in a posh Trinidad Embassy vehicle and after the ceremony there was a shortage of vehicles to take the guests to Crosby Hall, three miles away. One of my longstanding friends from our school days, Maurice Leppard, the former chief reporter of the Isle of Wight County Press, still one of Britain's bestselling local newspapers, and his wife Pamela were given a lift in the official car. Maurice, now eighty-three, said, 'I'll never forget that. Learie made us so welcome. He had no side about him. Marvellous man. I knew all about him because a wonderful Sunday School teacher Fred White in Wroxall, in the Isle of Wight, told us about this remarkable man. He said he wasn't just a great cricketer but a brave man who stood up against a lot of criticism from bigots at a time when black people weren't welcomed in England.'

It was so sad that Learie died four years later and Norma passed away two months later. He died of a heart attack in 1971 at the young age of sixty-nine and Norma was a victim of that cruel disease, cancer. They were lifelong sweethearts and when Learie died, she was heartbroken. Gloria, their daughter, was asked if she thought her mother died of a broken heart; she replied, 'Yes, partly, but the cancer was very advanced.' Our family lost a wonderful pair of godparents.

Back to the real cricket, the Test match series between England and the West Indies. There had been plenty of talk about the bowling of Charlie Griffith who routed England with his unusual yorkers and short-pitched deliveries in 1963, with Ted Dexter, Ken Barrington and the Australian skipper Bobby Simpson putting their names to critical articles on his bowling action. Simpson was hired by the *Evening Standard* three years later and Dexter and Barrington joined in the campaign to get Charlie banned. Barrington said, 'You are out there up against straight fast bowling on a length and suddenly the next ball, delivered from a suddenly straightened arm, comes in like a rocket and you can't pick it up. He should be no-balled.'

Learie replied to the critics in a frank and honest article under a headline 'Not Guilty Verdict on Griffith.' It said, 'The case against Charlie Griffith has been dismissed. And I hope that there is now an end to the controversy about the West Indian fast bowler's action, and that he is allowed to go about his bowling without this chucking threat hanging over his head. Two Test umpires, Arthur Jepson and Fred Price, watched him bowl at Oxford on Saturday and they were satisfied with his action.

'The controversy intensified long before the tour began but after the evidence in his favour at Oxford I can see no point continuing it. If Griffith chucks the odd ball in future matches and the umpires discover them it is the business of the umpire to no-ball him as he would any other bowler and leave it at that. But I do not think Griffith has much to worry about now that he has passed this test. He controls the ball better than any other bowler in the West Indian side and even if he is half as successful as he was in 1963 – when he was top of his side's averages with 32 wickets at 16.20 apiece – the West Indies should walk away with the series. And I know Griffith has been very depressed about the whole affair. And I know he was hurt by something I wrote recently – when I said I did not like his action as I thought it was an ugly action but this was an honest view and it was said without rancour and discrimination. I said let the umpires judge. Well, they judged at The Parks and found him not guilty.'

The downhearted Griffith also had problems with his front foot, conceding too many no-balls, in the Lord's Test and with his confidence shattered he finished the series with 14 wickets at 31.28 apiece. And he wasn't no-balled in the five Tests for throwing. 'After that, my career ended with having played only 28 Tests,' he said. Like most controversies in sport, the greatest amount of the publicity aimed against an individual overshadows the views of those who support him and Learie was on his own, calling on the critics to lay off Griffith.

The biggest loss for English cricket at that time was the sad end of Barrington's career. Wracked by anxiety, partly inhibited on by the Griffith issue, he asked to withdraw from the series and go on holiday. The team management agreed and he and his wife Ann spent a week in Bournemouth. He was never the same player and retired in 1968.

In the previous year Barrington – who started as an aggressive batsman and was criticised for it and became a cautious batsman – reached another crisis in the Second Test against a weak Pakistan team at Trent Bridge. The weather was poor and the pitch was helpful to medium-fast bowlers from the start. Hanif Mohammad (1934–2016), the then world record holder of the highest first-class innings of 499, followed up with the slowest Test innings, 337 in sixteen hours, faced 27 balls to score just four in the Pakistan's innings of 140 off 69 overs. England responded with 258–8 in tricky conditions and Barrington was 109 not out off 366 deliveries. Pakistan batted again and Derek Underwood (5–52) shot them out for 144, and Pakistan lost by 10 wickets. This time Hanif, the 'Little Master', mustered just 16 runs off 98 deliveries.

Horlicks sponsored the series and a panel of Brian Johnston, the Pakistan manager I.A. Khan, Horlicks director Reg Bowden and Learie had a short meeting to pick the Best Batsman. The first three voted for Barrington but in Learie's column he refused to vote for him. 'If you can't score quicker against a weak team when you are on top, what hope is there? I warn cricket's rulers that if the same thing happens in the final Test at the Oval then they must not complain when the public decide not to buy tickets.'

Poor Barrington was livid. 'Flippin' hell, he said, 'someone had to stay there and we did win the match.' Kenny rarely slept while appearing in Tests. Many cricketers have problems with sleeping but he was one of the worst.

England had been humiliated in the First Test at Old Trafford and Learie was scathing. In his summing up he said in his column: 'Unlike soccer, for instance, cricket is a game where defence cannot win. It can only avoid defeat. Cricket is an attacking game and the attacking side nearly always wins. Defence, when defence is called for, yes, but in English cricket in recent years there has been an obsession with playing safety first cricket. The refusal to take the calculated risk is a negation of the true spirit of cricket. Take the challenge out of cricket the game will die. The county championship is on its last legs and

I can see only weekend cricket in future. The cricket we have seen will be no loss to the game. I have thought that England players seemed to make hard work of what should have been a light-hearted task. In short, they did not give the impression of enjoying the game.'

He was right: I sat down with some players of the time and they were angry about his comments. One said, 'He might have been an exciting League cricketer for Nelson but his batting average in Tests was 19.24 and his first-class innings average was 24.05. Who is he to talk?'

That figure of 19.24 kept coming up in his life. As he explained, 'Being the wrong colour and I wasn't considered as a possible captain of the West Indies when captains were all white and many weren't Test standard. Then WW2 came and when it ended I was too old to play international cricket.'

Looking back after fifty years, Learie's forecasts about how the series went were eerily correct. Before the Lord's Test he said of Mike Smith, the England captain, 'His position must be in the balance. The fact that he is top of the county batting averages means nothing in Tests. The West Indies has his measure. Personally I don't give the job back to Cowdrey. He is of he same defensive mould as Smith and there should be a more positive approach. The man I am thinking about is Brian Close of Yorkshire. He is a man who believes in taking the calculated risk.'

Smith was sacked although Cowdrey was reappointed captain before the selectors called up Close for the Oval Test. With an ultra positive approach, Close led England to a famous victory. Learie also called for a recall for Tom Graveney: he was brought back after a long absence to score his 108th century, 109.

Interviewed at Wormsley in July, 2016, Mike Smith was asked if Learie was right. 'Yes,' he said, 'at that time we were too cautious. We should have swung the bat more and taken the initiative, like the West Indies did, particularly Gary Sobers.'

One of the most pungent articles Learie wrote was on St. Valentine's Day, 1968 when rioters threw bottles and tried to invade the pitch in the Second Test against England at Kingston, Jamaica. He wrote it himself and wired it over to Carmelite House. It came from the heart.

He said, 'Today I am ashamed to be a West Indian. I am ashamed because our good name as sportsmen has been cast down into the gutter all because of the actions of a few hundred hooligans. I would like to make excuses. I would like to say that the rioters who threw bottles at England's captain Colin Cowdrey were just ignorant louts who have no business in the ground in the first place. But what sort of excuse is ignorance? This was wilful violence, as ugly as the violence seen at some football matches and I hold no brief for violence, no matter what colour the skins of those who practice it may be.

'No, I make no excuses for the humiliation I felt as I watched police use tear gas to break up these hotheads. What I would do, and what I think is now necessary, is at least to offer the rest of the world some explanation for this apparently senseless outbreak. I know these fans on the popular side of the ground. I know the sort of shanties in which they live out their humdrum lives. They are deprived economically and emotionally. Their one source of joy is cricket. It sets them alight. Watch them arrive with a bottle of beer in their hands and not much in their heads but the idea that now they can really let themselves go and you can almost feel their tension and excitement.

'They roar and shout. They bet on anything and everything. Who'll get the next wicket? Who'll get the first six? They are as volatile as dynamite and the seven feet high fence that keeps them from exploding on to the pitch is there because the West Indian authorities have long recognised that these fans are potentially dangerous. When their bets come unstuck and their heroes fall, they are mad, really mad. They idolise gods like Basil Butcher and Gary Sobers. The thought of those gods being "given out" is enough to turn their cheers to fury.

'That's why, when Basil Butcher was brilliantly and fairly caught by England's Jim Parks, they refused to accept it. "Cheats," they yelled. "Cheats." But it was really they who felt cheated and robbed and that is something they feel for much of the time. Yesterday England denied them victory and the fact that the umpire who gave Butcher out is half Chinese added to their fury. Oh yes, coloured people can be just as racialist as whites when they are looking round for a scapegoat upon whom they vent their frustrated rage.

'It not only made me ashamed and sad and I can come away from the ground in the knowledge that the bitterness of one day soured this whole series. Of course it must not be allowed to happen again. The authorities must ban the taking of bottles into the ground and arrest offenders. There must be more police. Yet I fear any measures can only prevent rather than cure the wild violence we saw here yesterday. There may be remorse in many a West Indian heart this morning but the underlying ugliness that has expressed itself in Kingston will not be easily assuaged.

'As long as cricket remains an only chance for joy in joyless, despairing lives the risks of further rioting will persist whenever that joy is thwarted.'

Brian Close should have been captain on that tour but was sacked by the MCC for ill discipline at a match at Warwickshire the previous season. The publisher Stanley Paul signed him up to compile a ghostwritten day-to-day report for a book and Close said of the riot 'Bravely Colin Cowdrey had gone to the six feet high wire fencing and pleaded with the crowd to calm down despite the flying bottles. With Colin's intervention, backed up by Sobers' confirming that Butcher's catch was clean and the action of the England players picking up the bottles, peace seemed to have been restored. Play could have started but a riot squad arrived with steel helmets and shields and they only served to raise the crowd to fury. Bottles came over thick and fast and Cowdrey was left with no alternative but to lead his team from the field. Within seconds, clouds of tear gas swept over the area, causing men, women and children to flee in panic. The players were gasping for breath in the dressing rooms.' Play was abandoned and a sixth day was added and England, 68–8, was lucky to draw.

The story about the riot led the front page of the *Daily Telegraph* – a first time for cricket – and their heavyweight cricket correspondent E.W. Jim Swanton described it as 'the worst I encountered.' The wind was blowing the wrong way and the tear gas even interrupted a meeting of the Jamaican Cabinet meeting half a mile away. Another cricketing first was Kingston's ground being provided with air conditioning in their press box and though the journalists were able to write their reports without being tear-gassed, the transmission of the copy was held up because the Cable and Wireless operators were suffering the effects of tear gas standing outside the press box.

The late Sir Michael Manley, twice Prime Minister of Jamaica (1972–80 and 1989–92) and a friend of Learie's, gave only two paragraphs to the riot in his award-winning book *A History of West Indies Cricket*. He wrote, 'Douglas Sang Hue, one of the best of West Indian umpires, gave a correct decision but that did not avert the wrath that followed. For 75 minutes the rioting was totally out of control. Indeed, when play was finally continued, it was decided to add the 75 minutes on an extra sixth day.

'English cricket writers took the view that the English side was shaken and dispirited by the riot, the third in the West Indies in a depressingly short period of time. On the other side Sobers proceeded to give one of those performances on a nightmare pitch that set him aside as a player, completely extraordinary in the history of the game (*sic*).'

In his first spell as prime minister Manley led a moderately successful campaign that partly reduced the number of deaths caused by shooting in his country but the problem still remains. Educated in the London School of Economics, he was son of a former prime minister named Norman and married five women and had five children.

At Port of Spain in the Second Test, Sobers set a ridiculously generous target on the final day and England won the series 1–0 after he admitted, 'I'm probably the most hated man in Trinidad for declaring now but someone had to liven things up.' Learie joined in the chorus of protest. 'Gary went too far on that,' he said.

In May of the same year Learie approved the decision to give the captaincy to Cowdrey in the home Ashes series and wrote, 'The selectors would have been crazy to think of any other candidate.' There was no reprieve for Close and with no one with much experience, the selectors had an easy decision. Before the First Test at Old Trafford Learie wrote that Surrey's charismatic Pat Pocock was developing into another Jim Laker. After failing to take a wicket in the first innings Pocock took 6–79 in the second… and was promptly dropped for the rest of the series.

Before the Fourth Test at Headingly Learie was lamenting about the lack of talent in English cricket. 'The average age of the current England team is 31,' he said. 'Whereas players are blooded at a young age in the West Indies and Australia, here they are usually halfway to their dotage before they are given a chance. Young men have the boldness of youth. They take risks because they have no fear. Once a youngster comes into county cricket the trade union rules take over. His left foot goes down the line, defending, not attacking. This is the root cause of the illness in county cricket. This is why the game has been going to the dogs.'

Learie always drew a large postbag of complainants. That is a good sign of a provocative sports commentator who attracts attention and starts a debate. Geoffrey Boycott is still a master of it. A man from Hall Green, Birmingham, wrote saying, 'Just how much longer have we to suffer dreary Sir Learie? He is not only anti-England. He's anti-everything. What a statement to make: "England don't deserve to win." Who should have won then? Let us have a reporter with a fair-minded approach who will give a little credit where it is due. I want a fair report on what has happened, not what would have happened, or what they should have done, or what he would have done.'

A Mr Sacre from Catford, SE6, wrote, 'So England didn't deserve to win! Come off it Sir Learie! Our chaps in the last two Tests have given the game all they have got. You accuse the England batsmen of slow scoring. If you were watching, you would have seen some good Aussie bowling and the finest fielding side we have seen for years. Why not give credit to a team that fought their way into a winning position on two occasions and were frustrated by the weather?'

A.J. Jordan of Orpington wrote under a headline 'What a Bore!' – 'Was the *Sketch* right in commissioning Sir Learie to report on the Tests? I'd put him out! No matter what England or Colin Cowdrey may do, all one reads in Sir Learie's column is carping criticism. He is fast becoming the biggest bore in cricket.'

Learie responded with an honest assessment of his reasons for making criticisms of the England team. 'It seems I have upset some readers but I do not apologise for that. Let us get one thing straight. I am not anti-England or anti-anyone. Only anti-bad cricket. England has good players and they have played some good cricket. But they still cannot escape the shackles of defensive cricket which has dragged down county cricket over the years.

'I am not one who advocates that every ball must be hit for six or four as some people think. No other sport to my knowledge has had to call all its professional performers together and tell them quite bluntly that they were killing the game. I agree with Tom Graveney when he says there is too much county cricket. It is nonsense to expect a player to go all out every day of the week. Notice how overseas players usually score more and quicker runs in county cricket than the average English player. They are less inhibited.'

Earlier in 1969 Ken Barrington was hired by the *Sketch* to take over from Learie who by then had been made the first black lord to be honoured in the House of Lords, a governor of the BBC and was on several committees concerning race relations. His health had deteriorated and Barrington was less strident in his comments as a former player. Another favourable part of his appointment was that he was able to pass scoops to me! He was a lovely man who was loved by all, even Charlie Griffith when they met up in Barbados when he was coach to the England squad. They shook hands and the feud ended abruptly. Charlie said, 'All that criticism finished my career but I don't hold it against you Kenny.'

Barrington died of a massive heart attack on the England tour in 1981 to the West Indies in the Holiday Inn in Barbados, aged fifty. He was the tour manager and there was no cricketer of the time who was more popular. His humour and his malapropisms always brought smiles from his players and his loss dealt a severe blow to English cricket. His batting average for England was 58.07 and only Herbert Sutcliffe, with 60.73, and Eddie Paynter, with 59.67, bettered it.

TWO

DESCENDED FROM SLAVES

Trinidad had more slaves per acre in the middle of the 1800s – transported in inhuman conditions – than almost any other part of the Caribbean and Ali Pascall, a member of the Yoruba tribe in West Africa, was one of them. He was the maternal grandfather of Learie. Two authors, Gerald Malcolm David Howat (1928–2007), a cricket author, a historian and lecturer whom I met a number of occasions, and the *Guardian*'s Peter Mason published top class works on Learie including their valuable research into the extraordinary life of Ali, a Negro man who was unable to read and write. Gerald wrote thirteen books including much praised biographies of Walter Hammond, Plum Warner, Len Hutton and Learie and the last one, published in 1975, was awarded the Cricket Society's prize a year later.

His dealings with Learie were almost predestined because he was born in Glasgow and won a bursary at the cricketing school Glenalmond College near Perth and he first met Learie at the college when Learie was Rector of St. Andrews in 1968. The most startling coincidence came when Gerald taught at the oil firm Trinidad Leaseholds Ltd at Pointe-a-Pierre after WW2. Between 1926 and 1929 Learie worked for the same company, which enabled him to play more cricket. He was the highest paid cricketer in Britain in the 1930s and having rejected a job with the Leaseholds company in 1947 he finally returned to Trinidad in 1954 and became assistant legal advisor with Leaseholds and stayed there until 1961 when he returned to the UK to become High Commissioner for Trinidad and Tobago. Gerald must have been and gone when Learie was reinstated.

Howat's book entitled *Learie Constantine* started with the words 'Grandpa Ali Pascall was about a hundred years old when he died. His grandchildren took a last look at him in the open coffin, then they were lifted over it three times by their parents and told to go outside until the burial had taken place. Eight-year-old Learie asked why. "Because it was an African custom of the tribe grandpa came from," he was told. The child remembered the event vividly, for the funeral rites were lengthy, accompanied by wakes and vigils. Ali had started life owning nothing – not even himself – but he had become the caretaker of a few acres of a cocoa estate.'

According to Howat, Ali's parents came from the Niger Delta and had crossed the Atlantic in a slave ship – somewhat bigger than today's rubber boats taking thousands of migrants across the Mediterranean – and landed in Venezuela. Ali had become a child slave. They still have them in Nigeria. He knew a Negro girl named Malvina and together they stole a canoe and paddled across the seven miles to Maraval, a small village in Trinidad. Nearing the end of the journey the canoe overturned and they had to swim for the last mile or two. They lost all their meagre possessions. 'They were lucky to survive,' said Gloria, Learie's daughter and only child.

It was estimated that more than half a million Negro slaves were carried from Africa to the Caribbean from the early 1600s to 1807 when the English Parliament abolished slavery through the efforts of William Wilberforce, the Yorkshire philanthropist and humanist. It would have been more if hundreds of thousands had survived the rigours of the horrific journey. When the trade began, the owners paid around £7 for a slave but in Trinidad in 1813, when the authorities came in with a census, compensation claims were lodged with the British government for the loss of 17,539 slaves in the island when they were freed.

A report 'Slavery and the British Caribbean' said, 'Some experts believe that one of every three slaves died before they reached their departing African port. They felt alienated, fragile and thought that death was around the corner. The conditions suffered by slaves during the voyages were inhospitable to say the least. The slaves would be placed in close quarters, chained, fed barely enough to sustain them and often contracted disease. They were prone to weight loss and scurvy was common.' The skippers of the ships would give orders to throw the dead and near dead over the side.

Sugar was to blame for this: people in Europe wanted it to sweeten up their food and drink and rich ship owners, realising that almost all year 28–35°C sunshine in the Caribbean islands was ideal for sugar production. Some of the great public schools in Britain were financed by sugar entrepreneurs. A prominent one was Edward Colston, who started Colston's School in Bristol in 1710. He was an Anglican who barred anyone known as a Dissenter. In 2017 I went to Colston's to report on a cricket match between their first team with the Forty Club, whose members are well known for not showing dissent on the field.

Colston was a philanthropist as well as a slave owner and he financed several other buildings in Bristol and London including Colston Hall in Bristol, which is now renamed. There was a statue of him in Bristol and two roads were named after him. University students in Bristol wanted to remove reminders of Colston and were supported by others. Colston School was approached with a request to come up with another name but they resisted the idea.

In the aftermath of the death of George Floyd, when a US policeman kneeled on his neck causing Floyd's death on May 25th, 2020, people around the world reacted with angry demonstrations. Bristol took the lead in Britain and a group of activists put ropes around Colston's statue, yanked it over like Saddam Hussein's and took it to the River Avon and threw it in. The local mayor, Marvin Rees, the first black mayor in the history of the city, was embarrassed. 'I wanted to remove it for the past four years but that wasn't the way to do it,' he said. The council rescued the statue and it now rests in a museum.

One of the activists was the thirty-one-year-old Jen Reid, an associate of the sculptor Marc Quinn whose sculpture of a woman without arms – not hers – stood on a plinth in Trafalgar Square for some years. Quinn then proceeded to make a black sculpture of Ms Reid called A Surge of Power, which was put up where Colston's, which was Graded 11, stood. The council took it down and sent Quinn the bill for removing Ms. Reid's. Technically it is an offence to interfere with Graded buildings or statues.

Had Learie been alive he might have taken a more sensible view. Statues are built to thank generous philanthropists who remind a succession of generations they need people to be inspired to live a better life. Four centuries ago most rich men were cruel and avaricious, and life was generally cruel. In the late 1500s the African kings in West Africa were among the first to own slaves and when the first Portuguese explorers arrived they bought a quota off them. British ship owners, wanting cheap labour to cut the growing sugar crop in the Caribbean in the next century, bought more and more off them, and it was big business at the expense of up to one million Africans.

The habit of taking sugar more than 300 years ago was regarded as a healthy one. Coffee houses began in the mid 1650s to serve tea and it soon became the national drink, sweetened by sugar. In her book *The Hungry Empire* Lizzie Collingham said, 'It was a catalyst for Britain's growth into an industrial nation and for the enslavement of millions of West Africans, the results of which are still being felt. It was looked on as the opium of the masses. Feeding Britannia's sweet tooth was the start of the great British dental decay.' She quotes Aaron Thomas, a ship's purser in his sea diary at the end of the eighteenth century, 'I never will more drink sugar in my tea, for it is nothing but Negroes' blood.' But he was an exception.

The slaves worked punishingly hard through the waking hours in the Caribbean and when forced to slow down, by lack of vitamins, they would be whipped or flogged. They were poorly fed in the scorching sunshine and this contributed to low birth rates and the high mortality. Gloria spoke of her great-grandmother having ten miscarriages.

There were five children who survived in the Constantine family with Learie the eldest, born on September 21st, 1901. They were all Catholics and they remained in the Catholic faith. It was a big advantage to have an unusual name: everyone would remember it – Learie Nicholas Constantine. There were eleven Roman and Byzantine Emperors named Constantine and it is derived from Constans or Constanius, meaning 'constant, steadfast.' It is a common name in Greece and Cyprus. His family's name was thought to come from a French slave master Jean Baptiste Constantin. The name Learie came when Lebrun met a cricketing colleague in the UK, an Irishman by the name of O'Leary, and for some reason it was shortened.

The name of O'Leary originated in County Cork in South West Ireland in the eleventh century and it was used as a surname. Most of them migrated to the US. West Indians love finding exotic names for their children. Examples from a list of West Indian Test cricketers include Nyron Sultan Asgarali, Denis St. Eval Atkinson,

Sheik Fauod Ahumul Fasiel Bacchus, Eldine Ashworth Elderfield Baptiste, Nelson Betancourt, Sylvester Theophilus Clarke, Colin Everton Hunte Croft, Maurice Linton Churchill Foster, Berkeley Bertram McGarrell Gaskin, Lancelot Richard Gibbs, Alvin Ethelbert Greenidge, Cuthbert Gordon Greenidge, Conrad Cleophas Hunte, Hopnie Hobah Hines Johnson, Rohan Bholall Kanhai, Isaac Vivian Alexander Richards, Anderson Montgomery Everton Roberts, William Vincente Rodriguez, Cameron Wilberforce Smith, Garfield St. Aubrun Sobers, Everton de Courcy Weekes, Elquemedo Tonito Willet and finally Frank Mortimer Maglinne Worrell, the greatest captain of the West Indies.

But there was only one Learie.

Two years earlier Anaise Pascall, daughter of slaves, married Lebrun Constantine, a grandson of slaves. Lebrun was born in Diego Martin in the north-west of Trinidad on May 25th, 1874, not far from Maraval, which was founded by the Spanish. A family called Begorrats, wealthy slave owners, were Catholics and they built the first Roman Catholic church. For many years the black people were looked down on by the whites, who were many, mixed-race people and later, the Indians. Lebrun's grandparents were among the last slaves to cross the Atlantic and became a freeman and a freewoman after slavery was finally brought to an end in the British Empire in Trinidad in 1834. Unlike Barbados and Jamaica, where slavery lasted for a long time, it only lasted forty years in Trinidad.

The country was taken over by the British in 1797 and the new masters brought the sport of cricket, which had soon spread to the other parts of the Caribbean. It soon became the most popular sport in the region, preaching good manners and good habits. It introduced sportsmanship and it was carried through the centuries. Fortunately, it still survives. The names of the local cricketing heroes are still revered. Lebrun (1874–1942) was one of the pioneers. He was the first black man to represent Trinidad in 1895 and was of the first to be chosen by the West Indies two years later. Anaise's brother Victor Pascall (1886–1930) played for the West Indies as a slow bowler before they were given Test status. His first-class record of 171 wickets was a good one but his batting one – 859 runs at 13.63 – was poor.

Lebrun was affectionately called 'Old Cons' and was a far better cricketer. He was one of the lynchpins of the West Indies touring side in England in 1900 and 1906. In the first tour he had to give up his job as a cocoa overseer in Cascade and managed enough money to pay his expenses. He made only one hundred but his career 2,433 first-class runs at 25.34 was very respectable.

He built a matting wicket called the 'Constantine pitch' when the family moved to St. Ann's where Learie was ready to start at St. Ann's Government School primary school. There were three brothers, Osmund, Rodney and Elias, and a sister, Leonara, in the Constantine family; Rodney, a highly promising cricketer, died from typhoid at the age of twenty-two. Anaise had five miscarriages. She often kept wicket during the nightly sessions and also Leonara did as well. Osmund, who became a building contractor, kept wicket and Elias played for Trinidad between 1932 and 1949. His fielding was good enough to be picked as twelfth man for a Test, and he scored 895 runs at 27.12 and took 24 wickets at 36.33. He died on his ninety-first birthday.

With all this cricketing talent at hand it wasn't a surprise that Learie became a worldwide star. Peter Mason quoted him saying, 'My father kept us at it every spare moment of daylight. He was a martinet. If one ball got away from you and another followed he would give you a rap on he head.' Both the parents were hard taskmasters in all areas, not just cricket. They laid down a strong moral code. Learie was once beaten by his mother for stealing an egg he found in a ditch but by his own account 'they were fair and loving within the harsh strictures of the day, emphasising decency and good manners at all time.'

Learie said years later, 'A happy childhood is one of the greatest defences a man can have against the world. Our beloved cricketing sessions in the backyard and the strong values that surrounded them served as a cushion, I am sure, for the sterner life which was ahead for all of us. Even the washing-up was made fun. Dishes were used for catching practice. When we finished a meal my brothers would stand on the kitchen steps and I would be in the dining room and I would throw all the plates, crockery and cutlery to them.'

The idea that someone would be given a smack on the head from his parents caused no problems. In today's modern Britain the victim of it may well call ChildLine and make an official complaint, leading to a possible court case. In his book *Cricketers' Cricket* published in 1949 Learie wrote, 'I had to learn the hard way. Whenever I dropped a catch, or sent down a loose ball, got bowled or caught, he would rap me on the head with his knuckles. My head was hard but his knuckles were harder. He would say, "Pay attention Learie – that is how you learn cricket, by paying attention." I think it is the same with all sports, professions, and businesses whatsoever. Pay attention and you command success.'

Lebrun started out as a young cricketer by carving his own bat from coconut trees and using a lime or an orange as a ball. He formed his own side against village sides and at the age of twenty he led it to win a local competition. A year later he was chosen to play for Trinidad against an English amateur side led by R. Slade Lucas. In 1900 he joined the first West Indian tour to England under R.S.A. Warner, brother of Pelham, sons of Charles Warner, the Attorney-General of Trinidad. Sir Pelham Francis Warner (1873–1963) was born in Trinidad and the Constantines, father Lebrun and son Learie, became firm friends of the Warners.

Sir Pelham was known as Plum and was described as the genteel knight. He skippered Middlesex and England (fifteen

Tests averaging 23.92), managed the England side in the Bodyline tour in 1932–3, was cricket correspondent of the *Morning Post*, founded the *Cricketer*, carried his bat with 132 out of 237 on his Test debut and when he died at 89 his ashes were scattered at Lord's. Later in that tour Lebrun, coming in at number nine in the West Indian second innings, scored 113 at Lord's in a losing cause. Plum called it 'a dashing and faultless display.'

When Learie was born Lebrun's boss Sidney Smith, a white man, was asked to become the godfather. In 1906 Lebrun was wanted to play for the West Indies in the coming tour of England but he declined saying he didn't have the money, through losing six months' work. The ship carrying the players had just left the harbour in Port of Spain when a rich merchant named Michael Maillard volunteered to pay for Lebrun's gear and expenses. His benefactor chartered a motorboat for Lebrun to catch up the steamer in the Bocas Straits. Subsequently Maillard helped the expenses of both Lebrun and Learie when they toured the UK.

The first tour by the West Indies took place six years earlier after the autocratic Lord Hawke had skippered an MCC side in the Caribbean and was so impressed by the rising standards he persuaded MCC to accept a West Indian tour of England. Harold Austin was appointed captain but was called up to fight in the Boer War in South Africa. Aucher Warner, one of many siblings of Pelham Warner who later became Attorney-General of Trinidad, took over. Aucher soon contacted malaria and he only appeared in six matches. Joe 'Float' Woods, a medium-fast pace bowler, took over.

Crushing defeats against W.G. Grace's London County side, Worcestershire and Warwickshire, led to doubts about whether the tourists were good enough but against a Lord Harris's team at Lord's Lebrun dispelled the gloom. West Indies were 132–8 up against a MCC total of 395 when Tommie Burton, who had been born to an elite father and black mother in Barbados and was a clever medium-pace bowler, joined Lebrun and they opened up a barrage of stunning shots that put on 162 runs in only 60 minutes with Lebrun, 113, becoming the first West Indian to score a century in England.

Burton dismissed W.G. twice and bowled out Norfolk for 32 with startling figures of 8–9. But his career was brought to a permanent halt after he refused to clean the boots and cricket bats of the white members of the 1906 touring side. He moved to Panama and never played again.

Lebrun scored a half century at Gloucestershire and was overshadowed by Gilbert Jessop's 157 in only an hour and Woods found himself conceding five fours in an over. The issue of race was raised by Pelham Warner who wrote in his newspaper column, 'The black members were so amused that they sat down and shouted with laughter at the unfortunate bowler's discomfiture.' Feeling sorry for the bedraggled team, he volunteered to play for them. He turned out against Leicestershire and his century helped his adopted side to win by an innings. With Pelham not being available for more matches, further disasters followed: Nottinghamshire and even Wiltshire outplayed them without Warner.

Their record was five wins, eight loses and four draws. Lebrun finished with 610 runs and was second to Charlie Olivierre, a black middle-order batsman from St. Vincent. Charlie was one of the first West Indians to earn a living in England with Derbyshire and Yorkshire Leagues sides.

Cricket was the motivating force of the Constantines and Learie's natural assets and enthusiasm led to a sporting career as opposed to an academic one. He went on to attend St. Ann's Roman Catholic school between 1914–17 and there was no prospect of him being giving a scholarship towards undergoing further education. He became a useful footballer and a sprinter and captained the school first team for two years only losing once, to a team called Tranquillity of older boys who wore white trousers and boots whereas St. Ann's were attired with khaki shorts and black shoes.

He built up a reputation as a sprinter and a footballer with the talent to go further in these sports. But cricket was his passion. Besides his father and uncle Victor he had another cricketing mentor in Andrew de Four, the headmaster at St. Ann's. Typically West Indian, de Four told him to hit the ball and be adventurous. He followed that strategy throughout his career, which often cost his wicket through his rashness.

He left school aged fifteen and was too young to be called up to serve in the West Indies Regiment. He took a job as office boy in a solicitor's firm of Jonathan Ryan in the centre of Port of Spain and spent five years there. He found it unexciting preparing summonses, taking down statements and typing up the notes. He signed up with the Contaste School of Commerce, sitting in a room mainly among girls. Soon his typing speed reached a fast pace, often outdoing the girl's. He also learned how to service the typewriter which he used.

It wasn't a wholly sedentary job because he had to go to different courts and various offices and frequently sprinted from place to place to maintain his fitness ready for cricket matches. The chief benefit of the job was being able to leave the office around 4pm early enough to enable him to practise in the nets before the light faded from 6pm onwards. Floodlights hadn't been invented then, of course. It took almost a century before they were constructed at the Queen's Park ground. His weekly wage was fifteen shillings and he gave most of it to his mother for his keep.

For a while Lebrun and his headmaster told him not to play in senior cricket but things soon changed when he was picked for Lebrun's club Victoria, patriotically named after Queen Victoria, against the oddly named Stingo CC, an all-black side which featured two international stars, George John and Joe Small. The name of Victoria was changed to Shannon, and the club was predominated by black players and the matches at the Savannah, the massive open space in Port of Spain where the annual Carnival is still held each February, drew large numbers of spectators. Up to thirty matches were held on the same day. The players changed under trees. There were no grand pavilions. Most of the pitches were made of concrete, covered by coconut matting, very helpful to quick bowling. The blazing sun burnt the grass and the outfields were treacherous. Yet Lebrun's Shannon emerged as the leading club in Trinidad and produced most of the international players.

C.L.R. James, who became one of Learie's best and longest-standing friends, described the aggressive John as 'a formidable fast bowler. He was more than that. He was a formidable man.' Small played in three Tests and he was also a fearsome opponent for a teenaged Learie just about to branch out to become a real cricketer. The youngster succeeded to impress, especially with his electric fielding.

James was born in 1901, seven months before Learie was born and in his classic book *Beyond the Boundary* first published in 1963 and reprinted in 2005, he wrote, 'I saw him for the first time in 1911, a thickset, rather slow boy. He came to my father's school in St. Ann's for a short while. He was already known as his father's son. What I distinctly recall is that in the scramble for the ball he rather stood aside and watched "pass out" in the school yard. I did not know that already his father was coaching him and this rough and tumble probably did not appeal to him. My father's school was a government school, non-denominational. Learie was a Catholic and he soon left to go to a Catholic school.

'I lost sight of him for some years until about the early twenties when I was playing first-class cricket for Maple and he for Shannon. He bowled at me in a match, fast straight stuff to which one could play forward comfortably. He began to get wickets, make a few runs and, above all, take some catches. Even to my interested eye he was full of promise, but not more.

'Major Bertie Harrigan, however, was captaining Trinidad in the evening of his cricketing days. He knew a cricketer when he saw one and he probably could see much of the father in the son. Practically on his own individual judgment he put Learie in the inter-colonial tournament in 1921. But for the Major's sharp eye and authority it is most unlikely that he would have got in so early. Apart from a wonderful left-handed catch in the slips, he did nothing useful. In his only innings he tried a mighty swipe at, I believe, his first ball and was caught at deep point for nought.

'Thus the heir apparent to his father was godfathered by the most respected and influential cricketers in the island. From the very beginning he felt himself as good as anyone. This was a West Indian black man, of the lower middle class, but a man of conscious status. John, belligerent, announced that when he met the new star in the club competition he was going to send his wickets flying and all turned up to see. Constantine has described his innings more than once – 67 in an hour, composed of fast bowling of classic defence and the most brilliant strokes against fast bowling of the highest class on a matting wicket in the Savannah.

'More remarkable than the innings was what followed. Nothing followed. Constantine never played another such innings until 1928 in England. In England or Australia such a display would have made him a rare batsman.'

This may well have been the early signs of his being too big for his boots, to quote a local colloquial cliché. It left a feeling of resentment among some of his fellow cricketers. Cyril Robert James – who later was always known as 'C.L.R.' – said of the Shannon team, 'It was not mere skill, they played as if they knew that their club represented the great mass of people on the island.

They said, "Here on the cricket field, if nowhere else, all in the island are equal.'" The matches were played over two weekends with two innings per side. On one occasion Learie was ill and there was no one good enough to stand in for him and he went in to bat and was dismissed first ball. Lebrun congratulated him for making the effort. James said of him, 'No one could appear to play more gaily, more spontaneously, more attractively than Constantine, yet he was a cricketer of concentrated passion.'

John Arlott rated *Beyond the Boundary* in the top three sports books of all time and fifty-four years after it was published we can ask, 'Was it really that good?' C.L.R.'s writing style was impressive but the first hundred pages abound with the word 'I' as he talks about his cricketing prowess. In the middle he writes eloquently about his West Indian cricketing heroes, including Learie. The final section is mainly about left-wing politics and his efforts to help emancipate the Negro. I met him a couple of times before he died at the age of eighty-eight living in a small flat near the Oval and this frail but still sparky man seemed to be suffering from Parkinson's disease. Whenever he picked up his cup of tea his hand shook and most of the tea spilled into a saucer. I asked someone who knew him and was told, 'His hand was shaking all through his life!' He had a turbulent life. Married three times, he had a son, lived in the US between 1939–53 before he was deported for his political beliefs and in his later years, he lived in England.

James sometimes advised Learie with his writings and influenced the national selectors to pick Learie while many others who had talent and were black were overlooked as white players were preferred. Learie resented this and agitated for change. It was a generation before a black captain was finally appointed in 1959 – the popular, relaxed Frank Worrell.

Learie turned up late for his debut at the Queen's Park Oval – the equivalent of Lord's – and Major Harrigan, skippering the side, had to reprimand him. Learie explained that he noticed the time of the start was wrongly reported in a newspaper, causing him to be late. Someone had taken over his position. 'It was one of the nastiest shocks I ever had in my life,' he said.

In 1921 he met a beautiful girl named Norma Agatha Cox. She had no interest in cricket and Learie didn't introduce her to his cricketing friends. Soon they tried to arrange dates and Norma told Graham Howat, 'Learie could only spare a few minutes. He was living in the country and I was in the city and his last train went about seven o'clock and after work he would go to the nets to practise. I was a very poor second to cricket.'

In his debut match against Barbados in the intercolonial tournament, he scored 0 and 24, took 2–44 off 21 overs and made catch at slip – not enough to earn headlines. He had a habit of throwing the ball up in the air after making a catch, to celebrate. But on this occasion he dropped the ball. The Major gave him another dressing-down. Rain prevented a result and the Trinidad squad had to catch the boat back home. He had to wait a year before his next appearance, against British Guiana in 1922. Lebrun, now forty-eight, was playing his final game, a rare instance of a father and son playing international cricket in the same match. His uncle Victor also played. Learie didn't distinguish himself with bat or ball but his sensational fielding in the covers earned him another call-up.

After three first-class matches, he was chosen for the 1923 tour to England. His career in the firm was blossoming and he joined Llewellyn Roberts, a bigger solicitors' practice. He chose cricket, and resigned his job. It was a huge gamble. Financially, he had precious little money to spend other than on essentials from his thirty shillings a week allowances.

THREE

OFF TO THE LAND OF THE FREE – ENGLAND

Not many young cricketers have given as much expert and strict advice as Learie and he was well prepared for his first tour to England in 1923. Those long hours on their home-made pitch near their house under the tutoring of his father Lebrun and his uncle Victor Pascall proved very rewarding. They preached the unorthodoxy as well as the straight bat of the English as personified by Plum Warner. There was a distinct difference: West Indian batsmen were willing to hit out from the first ball whereas Plum and his friends opted to play themselves in before taking any liberties. It was Boldness v Caution and both had drawbacks. In Learie's case, over-impetuosity. Some of his critics thought he should get rid of his reputation as a swiper.

Scyld Berry, the *Daily Telegraph*'s esteemed cricket correspondent, usually comes up with interesting sidelines in his columns and on June 7th, 2017 he said Learie may well have pioneered the scoop shot over the wicketkeeper's head. This is what he wrote: 'One shot of Jos Buttler (in his innings of 61 against New Zealand on the previous day) was a flabbergaster even by Buttler's standards, when he scooped a short ball from Trent Boult over his head for six. It sailed downwind – downriver too if a TV gantry had not got in the way. It is tempting to say it was unprecedented, but Learie Constantine, the original limited overs all-rounder from the West Indies who became a Lord, claimed to have scooped a bouncer over his head in the Oval Test of 1939.' There is no film recording of the incident but it would certainly have been an intended, authentic shot, not a mishit which often finishes up over the fine leg boundary.

Learie was twenty-one when he was selected for the 1923 tour after playing only three first-class matches. He was contemplating marriage and without a job, he had to rely on meagre expenses of thirty shillings a week in wet and windy England. The lofty H.G.B. Austin, recognised as the father of West Indian cricket in that era, recommended Learie to be selected, basically because of his masterly fielding. A white man, Harold Austin was West Indian skipper, a son of a bishop, a business tycoon, Senior Member for Bridgetown in the House of Representatives and as C.L.R wrote, 'he was a big fish in our Trinidad pond.'

The steamship *Intaba* carried bananas and the West Indies cricket squad from Port of Spain to Bristol and they had to put up with cramped conditions and, often, sea sickness. A photograph was taken at the West Indies Dock on arrival and all fifteen wore a variety of Homburg hats, first invented by Prussians, as well as warm clothes. The tallest was Austin who was wearing a white raincoat and, more significant, he was one of the eight white men alongside seven black men, all primarily bowlers. The black men did the heavy work.

C.L.R. wrote about Learie's performances in his first tour, 'He made useful runs, got useful wickets and Sidney Pardon (the

Times cricket correspondent and editor of *Wisden*) called him an 'amazingly good cover point.' Pelham Warner arranged for him to be coached at Lord's. And Jack Hobbs told him he was yards faster to the ball than anyone he had seen. He gave him some hints on technique and finesse, which he stored for future use. 'He is a success, but he hasn't yet set the Thames on fire, and, what is more, he didn't try to.'

It was the first West Indies tour of England for seventeen years and there was pressure on Austin and his players to make an impression. In the first six weeks the weather was awful, tipping down most days, and the players were left to their own devices. Learie wrote to friends and said, 'Day after day we were positively shivering, playing for hours in the damp and drizzle with scarcely a ray of sunlight. It was difficult to appreciate what that really meant for us. I shall never forget that so-called summer. The rigours of it robbed us of our captain, froze up poor George John's bowling, upset Victor Pascall, and chilled the rest of us into pessimism. Being naturally exuberant, we fought against it, but it lay in wait for us and the rain trickled down our necks, damped the clammy sweaters we tried to hide in, and made our wrinkling flesh creep. I recall miserable journeys in freezing trains from one damp hotel to another, dressing rooms with their own private chills laid on and afternoons in the field when it was impossible to pay attention because one kept thinking about overcoats.'

These comments were used in one of his books and it made his reputation as a writer. One can't imagine a current English captain like Joe Root, or even Michael Atherton, writing such expressive words about a tour. Before July the side managed to win five out of their twelve matches and Learie's 77 in 65 at the Parks against Oxford University lifted some of the gloom and the West Indies won by eight wickets.

Learie wrote, 'The wicket [he meant the pitch, a common mistake made even today!] was perfect, far different from the matting wicket on which I had played nearly all my cricket. I could come to meet the short ball and devote all my attention to hitting it as hard as I could. I could drive anything the smallest degree over pitched and late in the innings I was gliding from the off stump to leg.' That was a clear indication that he was one of the first cricketers to plant his right foot in or just outside the off stump and use the speed of the ball to guide it towards fine leg. Orthodox coaches like Pelham Warner always advised batsmen to drive through mid-off in the V, head over the ball, and not take chances to try to work the ball to leg. In today's cricket a growing number of batsmen use the steer to leg, especially in short-form cricket.

Gerald Howat summed up Learie's state of mind at the Parks: 'The contrast between Constantine sitting ill at ease and unsure of himself, an uneducated negro of twenty-one struggling to make something of his life and the suavity and self-confidence of Oxford undergraduates of the 1920s – young men of his own age but white, upper class or middle class background, assured, and contemptuous of the colonials. Constantine reacted in the only way for the moment open to him, by making runs.' There had been some banter from the undergraduates, the ones who survived the horrors of the Great War, at the expense of his team, but they ignored the taunts. Today someone would report it to the police and the offenders could find themselves being fined or even imprisoned.

In the next match, against Surrey at the Oval, spirits were heightened when the mighty Barbadian batsman George Challenor (1888–1947) scored 155 not out and 66 not out to help gain a 10 wicket victory over the fourth placed county. A teacher, Challenor influenced a young Frank Worrell and was one of the originators of the great West Indian batsmanship, according to

Christopher Martin-Jenkins. MCC were so impressed by him that he was promptly elected a member of the Club. The cricket correspondent of the *Morning Post* wrote, 'he is good enough for any Test side.'

As a result of their startling victory, Austin's team was invited to take on the H.D.G. Leveson-Gower's XI at the Scarborough Festival at the end of the season, which was always well attended by Yorkshire folk who knew their cricket. It turned out to be one of the most stirring comebacks in the 1923 cricket season. Constantine wrote, 'That was our last day's cricket in England and a side packed with England players only needed a mere 31 runs to win. No one gave us a chance but we took the field prepared to make the England eleven fight for every run.' Jack Hobbs, Greville Stevens, Ernest Tyldesley, Wilf Rhodes, Percy Chapman and Frank Mann fell before Johnny Douglas and Percy Fender scrambled home.

Learie almost crowed, saying, 'We felt we had put the West Indies on the road to parity with England, Australia and South Africa. Much was still to be done but we had laid a true foundation.' His overall contribution wasn't reflected by his statistics on the tour. He took 18 catches, some spectacular, scored 425 runs and captured 37 wickets. Pelham Warner described him as 'the finest fielder in the world.' He made a huge impression: a star in the making. A senior writer in the *Wisden Almanack* wrote, 'In the deep he picked up while going like a sprinter, and threw with explosive accuracy. Close to the wicket he was fearless and quick. Wherever he was posted he amazed everyone by his speed and certainty in making catches which seemed beyond him. His movement was so joyously fluid and, at need, acrobatic, that he might have been made of springs and rubber.

'His batting depended considerably upon the eye and is sometimes unorthodox to the point of spontaneous invention.

He loved hitting sixes. Though relatively short for a fast bowler at no more than five feet eleven, he was lithe, stocky but long armed and bowled with a bounding run, a high, smooth action and considerable pace.'

An author A.M. Clarke taught him how to balance by bending down to pick up an object from the floor on one foot before falling. Clarke thought he had a presence and certain dignity that endeared him to crowds. 'His appearance was striking: his big, loose frame around middle height, the bold sculpture of his face, the black lustrous eyes, direct and intense, the long dominating nose, the wide, sympathetic yet firm mouth, and the strong chin, all conveyed an irresistible impression of decisiveness and strength.' Neville Cardus, yet to emerge as the most admired cricket writer of his time, wouldn't have bettered that.

The tour of Austin's weary players lasted six months and they won six matches, lost seven and the rest of the twenty-one games were either drawn on curtailed by the weather. None of them came home rich but if they had image rights – like today's big earners of sportsmen – only one person would have deserved a considerable sum: Learie Constantine. He was the number one crowd-pleaser yet when he arrived home, he was virtually broke, with no job, and hardly any prospects. Two junior clerk posts filled some of his time but he found difficulty in even having interviews for jobs because white bosses wanted white workers, not black ones. He had to live with his parents in Arouca, outside the east of Port of Spain, to save money.

His cricketing exploits had made him more recognised and playing for Shannon CC he starred with a rapid not out 167 not out against Queen's Park, the MCC of Trinidad. He also made modest scores in the intercolonial tournaments in 1924 and 1925 and in the winter of 1925–6 Austin was instrumental to reward him with four matches for Trinidad and the West Indies against the MCC touring side. Again he failed to make large scores but his attitude and enthusiasm was clearly displayed.

In one match his enthusiasm went over the bounds of fair play and he was given a stern warning. Some of the MCC quicker bowlers tried to unsettle some of the West Indian batsmen with persistent short bowling. When the West Indies took the field Learie decided to try the same tactics and bombarded the MCC captain, the Hon Freddie Somerset Gough Calthorpe (1892–1935), with bouncers. He owned the land where Edgbaston's Test ground was built and was a distant relative of Henry Blofeld and H.D.G. Leveson-Gower. He was a wealthy amateur who owed his place in the England side to his social status more than his ability on the field. He was thirty-three at the time and had difficulty in getting out of the way to avoid being hit by Learie's thunderbolts. He was best known for his corkscrew run to the wicket with his medium pace bowling, not his batting. In his four Test appearances he only scored 129 runs with an average of 18.42.

At tea C.L.R. James and some of his team came into the home dressing room and said in an authoritative voice, 'Stop it, Learie!' Learie responded, 'What's wrong with you?' His friend said, 'That's not cricket. Do not bump the ball at that man. He is the captain of MCC, the captain of an English county and an English aristocrat. The bowling is obviously too fast for him and if you hit him and knock him down there will be a hell of a row and we don't want to see you in any such mess. Stop it!' Learie agreed to bowl properly.

In one match for Trinidad against British Guiana, J. St. F. Dare lifted the ball over Learie's head at cover thinking he would be safe but Learie leapt like a flying fish, turned and held the ball. Dare's comment was, 'he gave the impression of climbing an invisible ladder to get to the ball.'

Another opponent, the Sporting Club CC, was dismissed for seven with Learie taking most of the wickets. He explained, 'we wanted to attend a wedding at two o'clock and we made it with time to spare.'

One of Learie's teammates on the 1923 tour, Joe Small (1892–1958), was responsible for getting a proper job for him two years later. Joe was working as a stores clerk for Trinidad Leaseholds Ltd in Fyzabad in the south of Trinidad and recommended Learie to the owner, H.C.W. Johnson. Oil was discovered in the island in the middle of the nineteenth century but the company was only founded in 1886 and the oil boom started before the First World War. Joe was a tall, loose-limbed all-rounder who scored 776 runs for an average of 31.04 in the 1923 tour and took 50 wickets (average 18.59) in the 1928 tour to England. He was highly respected. Learie was hired as a machine-shop clerk and soon moved up to become a quantity stock account ledger clerk for a wage of £8 a month. One of the few perks was a free hot meal at midday but for the rest of the time the employees were expected to cook for themselves. Learie soon became proficient as a cook.

A colour bar of sorts was imposed although Johnson, a white South African, allowed time off for both white and black cricketers. He put Learie and Joe Small on half pay when they took time off to play representative cricket. There were two distinct groups, one black and the other white and light-skinned. After work Learie spent many hours improving his fitness. He lifted weights and used chest expanders to build his muscles, enabling him to bowl for longer periods. He played for the Forest Reserve team at outside right, relying on speed to outrun his opponents, and won a number of cups for winning several 100-yard sprints. On one occasion he beat Ben Sealey, the Trinidad champion sprinter.

Living so far away from Port of Spain, he was only able to play occasionally for his club Shannon and one of his colleagues, Reynold Dolly, wrote about one memorable match in which Learie starred. He said, 'His father, the redoubtable Lebrun Constantine, took the then invincible Shannon team to Siparia by train for the feast of La Divina Pastora and to play the local team. The home team made 205 runs and by a strategic prolongation of the lunch interval Shannon had only eighty minutes to make the runs before the last train left for Port of Spain. Learie implored his father to let him open the innings and with five minutes to spare Shannon won by seven wickets, Learie's contribution being 185 not out in 75 minutes.'

In 1927 he found himself being bullied by a boss who accused him of being slack with his work. He was so upset that he threatened to resign and drop out of an important Cup match later in the day. Someone higher in the ranks intervened and apologised and after the match was played he told him that he would be transferred to their Pointe-a-Pierre works closer to Port of Spain.

There was little chance of him becoming a professional cricketer in Trinidad and with hardly any money in his bank, proposing marriage to Norma was almost impossible at that time. A friend recalled, 'He didn't drink and after a match he would go to Pacheco's billiard saloon where he played pin-pool or snooker.' His dates with Norma were intermittent and she questioned whether he was suitable husband material. His first love appeared to be cricket, not her. He assured her that his life would be shared with her, and cricket, and she needed a lot of convincing. Finally she agreed and promised she would take more interest in his cricket.

Norma's father, Faustin, was a chemist and she was only seven when he died. She was intelligent with an independent mind, very pretty, and after six years of courtship, she accepted his proposal of marriage. They married on July 27th, 1927 at St. Patrick's Church. 'There was a small gathering,' said Gloria. 'In those days people couldn't afford to have a larger one. There was no honeymoon and afterwards they returned to Arouca where they stayed with the grandparents. Next day they went to work as usual.' It was a love story lasting forty-four years.

In the coming months they had to decide whether Learie should stay in Trinidad, in penury, or strike out and try to become a well-paid cricket professional in England. Norma supported him when he broached the subject of playing in England in one of the Northern Leagues. 'I did some hard thinking,' said Learie, 'and I set to work at my cricket, making myself fitter.' He had no personal trainer. He did it himself. His aim was to ensure a place in the 1928 tour to England with the West Indies side and despite having a moderate season with his club, he impressed the selectors in a match against Barbados in the Test match ground, which he called 'the greatest I've played in.' His contribution was only 11 and 13 and his three wickets cost 210 runs but his fielding played a key part in a match which produced 1,677 runs. Barbados was 400 behind on first innings and complied 726–7 in its second innings, winning by 125 runs.

His bowling was quicker and most hostile and in one trial match to pick the touring side he scored a quick-fire 63 and captured five wickets for 32. That sealed it: he was in the squad. In April his only child was born, Gloria Theresa Constantine, and the father wasn't there to see her again until six months later. He was on his way to England. Norma was staying with grandparents and she recalled much later, 'he would write regular letters but they took a long time to get them.' Both Learie and Norma would have liked more children but Gloria said, 'there were complications.'

The tipping point in his life was eloquently summed up by C.L.R. James when he said, 'He revolted against the revolting contrast between his first-class status as a cricketer and his third-class status as a man. The restraints imposed on him by social conditions in the West Indies had become intolerable and he decided to stand them no longer.' His aim was to become the first outstanding personable West Indian cricketer to earn a living playing professionally in the United Kingdom – a pioneer.

FOUR

LEARIE REACHES HIS PEAK

There are billions of statistics about cricket and it probably outstrips any other sport but one statistic is never set out – the age when a cricketer reaches a peak before his standards begin to fall. My submission is that Learie attained that status on his second tour to England in 1928 at the age of twenty-seven. The West Indies side was well beaten in their first official Test series against England and even Ireland and Wales beat them. But Learie was the person cricket-lovers wanted to see. His all-round talents earned admiration everywhere he went. His batting was exciting, if not erratic – he was now fit enough to bowl at a speed of around 85mph – and his fielding was sensational. The late Michael Manley, former prime minister of Jamaica, in his monumental history of West Indies cricket described his bowling as: 'as fast as anyone in the world.' As for his batting, 'he operated one way: attack. With a quick eye and supple wrists that are typical of the black exponents of the game in the West Indies he could take any attack apart. He could never do so for long periods because he did not permit himself the luxury of defence. But while his luck held, he could cut and hook and pull and glide and smack the ball through the covers with the best of them. He brought the nature of West Indian cricket to the world: good-natured aggressiveness, extrovert exuberance, panache.'

Sir Garfield Sobers, the greatest of all time, was generally thought of as being at his peak on the tour of England in 1966 when he scored 25% of his side's total number of runs, took almost 20% of the wickets and held the most catches, 10 in the five Test series which he led, and brought about a 3–1 win almost single-handed. He was twenty-nine. Brian Lara idolised Sir Garfield and he set out to keep the Test record of the highest individual score then held by Sobers, 365, in the Caribbean. He raised the bar to 375 on a flat pitch at the St. John's Recreation Ground in Antigua on 18th August, 1994 in 766 minutes, 538 balls, with 45 fours and no sixes. Ten years later he raised it again to 400 not out on another featherbed pitch in 778 minutes, 582 balls, 43 fours and four sixes on the same ground. Neither of these innings showed the true qualities of the man – which was playing dashing, glorious shots all around the wicket. In both times he did a Bradman: he accumulated.

But the innings he played at Sydney on January 5th, 1993 when he was twenty-four was his finest when he scored 277 runs off 372 balls with half the runs from boundaries. Bradman called it the best he had seen. Lara stayed close to his peak from then until his mid thirties before his sore knee and deteriorating physical state caught up with him. Both Sobers and Lara could take the attack to the opposing bowlers at will, using extravagant stroke play, even excelling Learie's ferocious way of batting. But they were able to play a more restrained innings when the situation called for it. In 1928 Learie showed off the best of his repertoire. He rarely kept it up though.

He was able to see his daughter Gloria for a week after her birth on April 28th and a few days later he set off for England.

Six months went by before he returned home to greet her. Did she recognise him? 'I suppose so,' she said, 'but my memory doesn't go back that far!'

His personal achievements on the field enabled his spirits to be maintained and boosted on the tour by reading Norma's frequent encouraging letters. The weather didn't help. The rain came down most weeks although the volume fell well short of the total of inches in the 1923 tour. The uncovered pitches – covers were universally adopted in the mid 1960s – were sluggish, unsuitable for their three genuinely fast bowlers, Francis and Griffith from Barbados, and Learie from Trinidad, who were brought up on hard, baked pitches with bounce. But when the sun came pitches were treacherous, almost exclusively helpful to spinners.

In the three Tests at Lords, Old Trafford and the Oval their three fast bowlers took a total of 22 wickets whereas the five-feet-two-inch-tall Alfred Percy 'Tich' Freeman, England's legendary leg-spinner, googly and topspin bowler, took the same total at a much lower cost of runs. England batted only once in each of the Tests and they won all three by margins of an innings of 58, 30 and 71 runs.

The tally of George Nathaniel Francis was six wickets, Herman Clarence Griffith's was 11 and Learie's only five. Francis, who died at the age of forty-five in1942, was the first great West Indian fast bowler to emerge from the Caribbean. The temperamental Griffith, who lived to eighty-seven, took the largest tally of 103 wickets on the 1928 tour. He was left out of the 1923 tour for disciplinary reasons and it was rumoured he was a communist. He was probably groomed by C.L.R. who was an admitted communist for much of his life. He bowled Don Bradman for 0 on the 1930–1 tour to Australia and he was fond of bringing up the subject, calling Bradman 'my rabbit'. Francis, a more relaxed, unemotional character, followed Learie to become a professional in league cricket in 1933 but wasn't successful playing for Radcliffe in the Bolton League.

Wisden Almanack had a doleful summing-up for the visit of the 1928 tourists – 'whatever the future may have in store the time is certainly not yet when they can hope to challenge England with a reasonable hope of success.' It would have been different had Learie maintained his exciting form against the counties. In the Tests, he took only five wickets at a cost of 52 runs and totted up only 89 runs in six innings.

It was tough that England had one of their strongest squads in its history while the West Indies was in an experimental period, nervously stepping out into the wide world: it was to be repeated eighty-nine years later in the 2017 tour. Captained by a debonair giant of a man, Percy Chapman (1900–1961) captured the imagination of the public and before he finally quit as captain in 1930 he had the confidence of his players. Latterly, excessive drinking was the cause for the premature ending of his reign. He had one of cricket's greatest opening partnership in Jack Hobbs and Herbert Sutcliffe, followed by the legendary Walter Hammond, ex-skipper Douglas Jardine and Ernest Tyldesley. Maurice Tate was in his prime as a medium-fast swing bowler and Harold Larwood was approaching his fastest speed, considerably faster than the West Indies trio.

At Derbyshire in the opening match the tourists needed 40 to win with two wickets remaining. Told by his captain to take no chances, Learie proceeded to hit five fours in a brief, mini hurricane innings which brought victory without losing another wicket. In one of his books, he wrote, 'I ought to be careful but I didn't feel careful. I had been watching the bowling and knew that the Lord had given it into mine hand.'

Essex was their next opposition and in bitterly cold weather at Leyton CC he scored a whirlwind 130 out of 190 in an hour and a half. The expenses of the tour weren't paid for by MCC, who was running cricket in England at the time. They were paid by a number of West Indian businessmen and with hardly any spectators at the early matches, there was a possibility they would withdraw their money. The pressure was on Learie and the other experienced players to do better. Against Surrey at the Oval he impressed the watchers scoring 50 in the first innings and 60 not out in the second.

Weather continued to chill the bones of the visitors and their first appearance at Lord's against MCC was restricted to 31 overs over the three days. His bowling found the target at Cambridge University when he took five wickets in each innings. Trying to find extra pace, he pulled a muscle and with the first Test at Lord's looming he faced a serious predicament: if he played half fit he risked being put out of action for the rest of the tour.

The following match was against Middlesex at Lord's and his chances of playing were minimal. Hot and cold towels were used on his leg: no electronic aids had yet been invented. He said on the eve of what turned out to be his greatest performance: 'I went up not too confidently for a medical examination and the doctor shook his head and told me not to touch a cricket ball for a week or ten days or I might do myself permanent harm. I knew the tour had failed to cover its costs. If we failed against Middlesex, interest in the Tests would be knocked to bits just at the time when our bright displays were raising everyone's hopes. Harry Mallett, the team manager, told me, "You are our draw card. If you drop out, we shan't do much business. But you must decide yourself. I don't want you to harm yourself." Well, it was my year and I would have to play. The doctor was summoned and told me it was up to me. I remember that June morning so well – the glorious heat of the sun, the tense expectancy, and the feeling in my bones that muscle or no muscle I would show them some cricket at Lord's. The doctor's face grew as long as my arm.

'He said, "It is my place to warn you that it is most unwise for you to play. Probably you will break down on the field and the consequences may be serious. You must make up your mind." "I'll play," I said. "You're mad," he said. But he gave me a great grin.' Learie announced that he would play and had a hot bath and a massage before the start.

In the absence of Francis, Karl Nunes, the captain, threw the ball to Learie to start the innings, and bowling from the pavilion end, his favourite end, he dismissed Harry Lee for seven. The rest of the day was dominated by Nigel Haig, with 119, Jack Hearne 75 and Patsy Hendren 65* and Learie dropped a catch in the slips off Hendren although *The Times* praised his overall fielding performance. A score of 313–6 on a sluggish pitch suggested that the tourists would be in line for yet another embarrassing defeat.

The contest had started on a Saturday and the next day was a rest day, giving Learie the chance to have more treatment and more hot baths. Hendren resumed on the Monday and scored the 38 more runs to reach his century before Frank Mann declared on 352. Learie's bowling was presentable but not menacing. By lunch the West Indies had sunk to 79–5, an abysmal performance. He came in at seven and strode to the middle glancing around the sparsely populated seats and standing areas. Bowling at the pavilion end was George Oswald Browning Allen (1902–1989), a remarkable man aged twenty-six who was born in Australia from English parents. Educated at Eton and an amateur player, Christopher Martin-Jenkins described his action with these words: 'attacking like "flaming fire" his right arm fast bowling with a sideways on action was touched with greatness; in measure he possessed rhythm and the ability to make the ball hurry off the pitch.' What happened now was in reverse – the ball hurried off Learie's bat.

His second ball was firmly driven for two and from his second over Allen went for a boundary through extra cover. The next delivery was struck with power for three. Soon Learie was in his 20s and the bombardment intensified. Allen tried a yorker and a scything swing of the bat sent the ball high into back of the Grandstand. It brought his score to 49. Watching in the pavilion was the then Lord Dunglass who became prime minister in 1963–4 and a President of MCC. He was better known as Sir Alec Douglas-Home and was a very capable cricketer. He said of Learie's extraordinary stroke: 'it was the best shot I ever saw from him, off a none too short ball which he sent to the feet of Father Time on the top of the Grandstand. It was prodigious.'

Next ball Learie glanced to leg for his first single in his sensational innings. It brought up the 50 off 22 deliveries in eighteen minutes. Today these totals and times are not uncommon, compiled by extremely strong men wielding heavy bats like Chris Gayle, Jos Buttler, Ben Stokes, Aaron Finch, A.V. De Villiers and others. In Learie's day the outstanding batsmen mainly used lightweight bats and were taught to play with a straight bat, restricting them to the V, guiding the ball through mid-on or mid-off, or sometimes straight past the bowler. There were no reverse sweeps, no ramp shots over the head.

The Middlesex leg break bowler Jack Hearne was brought on and he slowed Learie's scoring rate a little but the runs kept flowing. More and more MCC members arrived after hearing the news about Learie's feats. Mann called on one of Allen's friends, twenty-year-old Ian Alexander Ross Peebles, to bowl. Educated at Glasgow Academy and Oxford University, he was also tutored at the Aubrey Faulkner School of Cricket. He had a classical action with a deceptive googly and looping flight. That season he had experimented on his googly and with Learie scoring freely off his leg breaks, he tried a well-pitched-up one. Learie lashed out and missed – bowled for 86 in only 55 minutes. In that time only 11 more runs were added. He was like a one-man band and he left with a standing ovation all around the ground.

Another of the Middlesex fraternity, Plum Warner, said it was the finest display of hitting since Gilbert Jessop 'in more orthodox style.' Peebles took 100 wickets for Middlesex in the following season and his first-class total of 923 wickets cost a low average of 21.38. A gentle, gentlemanly man whom I met a few times when he was cricket correspondent of the *Morning Post*, he also wrote a large number of humorous books written with considerable style. That type of popular person with immaculate manners no longer survives in modern society – sadly.

Allen exerted great influence on cricket in his long and distinguished career. He was well known for refusing to bowl deliberate bouncers at the Australian batsmen in the Bodyline series in 1931–2 and I met him on a number occasions, usually for a ticking-off after writing what he thought were contentious articles in the defunct *Daily Sketch*. He wasn't the kind of man seeking favours. He was very forthright and opinionated. He was also renowned for saying he would never let the trees on the Nursery at Lord's be obscured by high-rise buildings in his lifetime and that was true. But recent plans at Lord's, not the building of high-rise flats but of two more tiers, will enable thousands more seats to be added at that end.

Allen's first-class career lasted from 1921 to 1954 and his statistics were impressive – 9,232 runs for an average of 28.76 and 785 wickets for 22.31 apiece. In his twenty-five Tests he made one century, scored 750 runs (24.19) and took 81 wickets at 29.37. All that work, particularly his fast bowling, caused him to have four hip replacements and not all of them were successful. He finished up walking with the aid of sticks.

His CV was overwhelming – captain of England and Middlesex, chairman of the Test selection panel, President of MCC in 1963–4 and treasurer from 1964 to 1976, all of these jobs wielding tremendous influence, and he was knighted in 1986 for his services to cricket.

Allen was universally known as 'Gubby' and lived a few yards from Lord's and the pavilion was reckoned to be his spiritual home. He never married. As a child born in Sydney he was originally known as 'Gobi' for his talkative conduct but when he moved to England it became 'Gubby.' He made plenty of enemies but like his great friend Jim Swanton, the long-time cricket correspondent of the *Daily Telegraph*, he was a stalwart supporter of the traditional virtues of the game. Reincarnated, he would certainly jump out of his grave today to see what was happening in T20 and blocking the trees at the far end of Lord's! Learie had great respect for him, especially as they were both fast bowlers and sloggers and there would be plenty of things to argue over. A televised crosstalk with the two of them would make a memorable programme.

The great Australian batsman Charles Macartney (1886–1958), known as the Governor General, was sitting in the crowd that day when Learie made his first innings 86 and he was reported to have said he was the hardest hitter of a cricket ball that he had seen. He had connections with Northern League people and it was he who later recommended Learie to play for Nelson. Besides his first-class 49 centuries and 419 wickets, bowling off a long run and bowling slow left arm, he once scored 345 in a day against Nottinghamshire.

Before play started, Macartney, a strict little man of five feet three inches who was a teetotaller and a Freemason, came up to Learie, shook hands and said, 'Mate, you are being too careful. Hit those bowlers!' After a short time when Learie had a sight of the ball he remembered Macartney's advice and started lashing out. 'There was a lump in my throat,' said Learie when he came up the steps of the pavilion. In his second innings, Macartney was waiting to clap him on the back and said, 'Remember what I told you.' He followed the advice and when he was out, after much cheering, he said, 'There are times that make life worth living.'

In his book *Cricketers Cricket* he wrote, 'It was Macartney who told me how to play "Tich" Freeman. A gnome of a man with a wonderful control of the ball was getting all of us out for small scores and we were beginning to develop a complex about him. We retired into our shells and he screwed us out with his leg breaks and sent us sadly back indoors. He said, "Take an over or two to get the feel of his bowling and then run right out to him and hit him and keep hitting him." It sounded terrifying but I did it and got some fast 50s against him while others were still retreating from him and getting pinked. Later I tried the same thing against Grimmett and Verity and others of the best.'

The West Indies score was 186 when Learie was out in the Middlesex match and only 44 more runs were added, leaving them 122. With half an hour's play remaining Learie and Francis bowled as fast as they could against Harry Lee (1890–1981) and Allen who volunteered to be the nightwatchman. Lee, who was injured and captured by Germans in the Great War, returned home with a limp and that didn't stop him becoming one of England's soundest openers. Learie was too fast for him, yet again, removing his middle stump. Lee had two other cricketing brothers. Jack was killed in action in 1944 and Frank (1905–1982) became a respected Test umpire who stood in twenty-nine Tests between 1949–1962. He was best known as the umpire who kept calling South Africa's quick bowler Geoff Griffin for throwing at Lord's in 1960. Griffin never recovered.

Allen didn't last too long as a nightwatchman. He took a severe blow to his unprotected chest from a bouncer bowled by Francis and, clearly unsettled, he lobbed the ball gently to the bowler. Middlesex came in 182 ahead with eight wickets down, relieved that it wasn't more than two down.

Patsy Hendren was soon struck on the chest by a short-pitched delivery from Learie next day and with his reputation, he probably wore a chest protector. He pioneered the idea of wearing a makeshift helmet and it took another generation before helmets were widely adopted. Joe Small removed Jack Hearne and the recalled Learie, at his most ferocious, shot out Haig and Killick after intimidating them with bouncers. Hendren was another victim, caught by Francis at slip. Peebles followed almost immediately, shell-shocked as Learie's yorker made a mess of his stumps.

Tailenders Price and Powell came and went, hapless victims of Learie and in 6.3 overs he had taken six wickets for just eleven runs and Middlesex tumbled from 100–3 to 136 all out. The odds were still on the home side because West Indies had to get 259 in 220 minutes and the pitch was breaking up. Roach was soon run out and Challender, on 33, departed after being unable to build a bridgehead. The tourists still needed 138 in 90 minutes when Learie marched in at seven. Peebles had the ball and, undeterred by losing his wicket in the first innings, Learie charged forward to drive his first ball to the long on boundary. Allen was still sore and unable to bowl and Durston, the faster of the bowlers, needed treatment on a shoulder. Haig was the only fit seamer.

Learie, realising that one mistake would end his side's chances, began keeping the ball down and scoring 'safe' runs rather than boundaries. The rate was still one a minute. When Jack 'Young' Hearne, the leg-spinner, dropped short Learie bent down on his left knee and smashed the ball with a horizontal bat dangerously close to Hearne's shoulder and hit the pavilion steps, just missing a group of startled MCC members. He was finding the range now, blasting a six. One pull, hit with great velocity, bounced off Hearne's bowling hand causing the injury which ended his season. It was brutal cricket.

Lee was a useful medium pacer – he took 376 first-class wickets – and was brought on to change the pace and line of the attack but except for one over he, too, came in for severe treatment. Learie was fast closing in on a century. He achieved it with a straight six. With five runs to win, he was out for 103, out of the 133 for the sixth wicket in just over an hour, with two sixes and twelve fours.

Another wicket fell but the necessary runs were obtained with three wickets remaining amidst rapturous cheers from the small contingent of West Indian supporters.

Learie was now on the front of cricket's stage – a superstar. The *Trinidad Guardian* brought out a special supplement to mark his performance. And the Fleet Street newspapers gave longer than usual reports of his marvellous all-round achievements. He acted like a West Indian hurricane, knocking everything in his way.

The three Test matches were almost a washout with the fledgling visitors brushed aside by a much more powerful and experienced team. Learie made some modest inroads in the opening Test at Lord's. He took the first wicket as a Test nation, dismissing Hallows at 51, and was the most successful bowler in England's 401 with 4–82. West Indies, despite not having to face the injured Larwood, collapsed at 177 and following on, they collapsed again to 55–6. On the final day they were hustled out by the spin bowlers Freeman with 4–37 and Jupp's 3–66 and lost by an innings and 58 runs.

Light relief came at Northamptonshire, one of the weakest of the counties, when Learie hit an almost one-a-minute 107 and captured a total of 13 wickets for 112 including a hat trick. West Indies won by an innings and 126 runs. A meeting at Stoke brought together Learie in opposition with the austere fifty-five-year-old Syd Barnes, still one of the greatest medium-fast bowlers of all time. Learie came on out top, bowling out Barnes cheaply in Staffordshire's 99. Learie made 38 out of his side's 159 and Staffordshire almost doubled their first innings total to 181. Barnes then removed Learie, not before he had passed 1,000 runs for the tour. The West Indies were cheered up by winning by eight wickets.

Warwickshire's formidable Robert Elliott Storey Wyatt (1901–1995), a cousin of the notorious MP and gossip Woodrow Wyatt, came under bumper attack by Learie in the match at Edgbaston. His balding head was struck twice in successive balls and he carried on without calling the trainer saying 'Fortunately they were glancing blows and didn't knock me over.' In a later Test against Australia, he was hit and injured but insisted on writing down a revised batting order before he was treated. He was a tough cookie! He was born in the same year as Learie and succeeded Percy Chapman as England captain in 1930.

Canon John Parsons won a Military Cross in the First World War and he, too, managed to stay on his feet without being hurt as the bumpers continued. With Learie resting, Parsons took revenge off the tourists' hitting spinner Scott for four successive sixes in his 161. One six broke the window of the tearoom, considerably reducing the number of cups and saucers available to be used: they were smashed to smithereens.

Learie came up with one of his specialist shorter innings, 70 in just 40 minutes. It wasn't enough: Warwickshire's Andrew Speed found himself surprised to take 9–99 and carry them to victory. Nunes's harassed men must have had a heavy night because Speed only played eight matches in all for Warwickshire before he retired.

In those days of uncovered pitches it was usual to bowl first. When the pitches dried, the ball (only used once per innings in county cricket) would leap up and often cause injury. For the Second Test, Nunes reckoned the pitch was too soggy for his bumper bowlers and decided to bat. As expected, the pitch dried quickly and Freeman with 5–54 and Jupp with 2–39 – the Lock and Laker of the 1920s – bowled out the tourists for 206.

Jack Hobbs was back after missing the First Test and he and Herbert Sutcliffe, the man with a posh voice, put on a century in the face of a rain of bumpers from Learie. Afterwards the

Master, as Hobbs was known, told a journalist that he didn't play cricket in order to get his head dented. Even in those days there was acrimonious sledging with Jardine heavily involved. He, too, complained about an excessive amount of short-pitched bowling.

Jardine (1900–1958) was at his peak, topping the national averages of 87.15 in 1928. He was heading for a century when he trod on his stumps and refused to leave the wicket. The West Indians were enraged; maybe not Learie, who didn't swear and hardly drank. Jardine claimed he had completed his shot before he stepped on to the stumps. The umpire accepted Jardine's opinion, bringing about more chirping from the fielders. Soon after, Learie ran him out with a marvellous throw and there was more patois abuse from the frustrated fielders. Percy Chapman became the next batsman to suffer inconvenience, retiring on three. A total of 351 should have been overtaken by the West Indies in their second innings but they subsided to 115, going down by an innings and 30 runs. Tich's figures were 18–5–39–5.

Morale was shattered and what they needed was a weekend in Blackpool enjoying themselves. Instead they were driven to Llandudno to take on a Wales team which contained the destructive Syd Barnes. In poor light Barnes whipped them out twice for low scores with a match-winning analysis of 12–138 and Wales claimed a famous triumph. Four dreary draws against Leicestershire, Somerset, Glamorgan and Gloucestershire followed, prolonging the boredom of shattered men who would prefer being at home in the Caribbean.

The final Test at the Oval was settled on the first day when the Nunes men capitulated to 238 on a typical flat, hard Oval pitch. Learie made his highest score in the Tests, just 37. The gentlemanly Hobbs (1882–1963) played one of his most attractive innings of 157, punishing Learie with his searing cover drives and cuts. Maurice Tate, who finished with seven wickets, even scored 54 in the total of 438. I once met Sir Jack Berry Hobbs, from a family of twelve in Cambridge, in his sports shop in Fleet Street round the corner from the *Daily Sketch* and he couldn't have been nicer. He gave me a good discount for a box of six balls. He was approaching his eightieth year and here he was still working away... and smiling.

Larwood, (1904–1995) with his long, bouncing run, softened up the visitors with his three wickets without hardly bowling short and Learie was caught by Larwood off the bowling of Maurice 'Chubby' Tate (1895–1956) for 17. Second time round the West Indies flopped to 129, ending up with another hiding, out for 129 in 72 overs. Awful!

Two charity matches dragged on into late August. Learie scored a rapid 62 against Sir Julien Cahn's XI at the Folkestone Festival and against the Leveson-Gower XI at packed Scarborough, Learie didn't let them down, knocking over seven wickets for 68 in the hosts' first innings. In response Sir Jack made an elegant 119 against Learie at his fastest.

England's senior players all agreed that Learie was on his way to greatness. He hardly missed a game. Despite his relatively poor figures in Tests, he was second in the averages with 1,381 runs at 34.52 and was top of the bowling averages with 107 wickets at 22.95, completing a rare double. He wanted a rest but more than that, he wanted to be with Norma and the daughter he hardly saw.

Stretched ahead was a tedious two-week sea journey back to Trinidad.

FIVE

THE KING OF NELSON SIGNS ON

During the Middlesex match three officials of Nelson Cricket Club in Lancashire went to see Learie about being appointed as their professional. The contact was set up by Charlie Macartney who had connections with their club. In 1928 there were no agents advising cricketers but the much-respected Charlie, rated just behind Don Bradman in cricketing stature and as a person, gave Learie and the Nelson officials plenty of helpful advice. Charlie told Learie to go high about a contract because he had box-office appeal.

The cricket club was almost broke in 1928 with debts totalling £3,000 but they were gambling on having a mercurial all-rounder who might win the hearts of cricket-lovers all round the nation. The then population of Nelson was 39,000 – now it is 29,000 – and many of them knew about his exploits and wanted to see him in action in person. Before returning to Trinidad he was offered a three-year contract at £500 per year, paid at £25 in weekly instalments to ensure that he and his wife Norma could pay the bills. They also offered him up to £100 each season in bonuses for reaching 50 and taking five wickets. They paid their fares to and from Trinidad as well. These riches – unheard of in domestic cricket at that time – made him the highest-paid cricketer of the day. To illustrate the fall in the value of the pound, in 2018 Learie would, had he attended a session as a Lord at the House of Lord's today, receive a daily allowance of £323 and up to £150 for travel outside of London. One day's work today equals his summer's remuneration in 1929. George Headley, revered as the Black Bradman, was paid £500 by Haslingden in 1934 but no one else came close to the sum paid to Learie.

Before signing the contract, Learie telephoned Norma in Port of Spain to ask what she thought. It would cause upheaval and she would miss her relatives, the almost perpetual sun and the annual Trinidad Carnival but she realised his chances of making a career in England – he wanted to qualify as a barrister – would be greatly enhanced. Playing only on Saturdays in the League, and confined just to Lancashire and not fagging around Britain playing six days a week, gave him a wonderful chance to study and live at a reasonably good standard. Calm and determined, Norma was the prop in their marriage and she gave her every encouragement. The deal was soon done.

The name Nelson was first mentioned in the early thirteenth century, a combination of the names of Nel and Eleanor. After the battle of Trafalgar in 1805 – an away win for England's Vice-Admiral Horatio Nelson – a vast number of hostelries in England were named after him. One of them, a coaching stop in the early 1800s, was situated in the area bordered by several villages, the biggest being Little Marsden and Great Marsden four miles north of Burnley.

Two outstanding engineering enterprises of the area were the Leeds–Liverpool canal in 1816 and the East Lancashire Railway in 1849 and they brought a great transformation. There was a Marsden station in Yorkshire and to avoid calling the new station the same name, the name of Nelson was selected. There was cheap land and stone in abundance and certainly plenty of cheap labour enabling the introduction of a number of mills. By 1921, 88.9% of the 17,299 adult population worked in weaving. This led to a powerful trade union and in 1905 and the late 1920s there were lockouts and the town was known as 'Little Moscow', implying communists and Trotskyites were influencing the workers to try and fight back against the mill-owning families.

By the time Learie arrived the mills were on the decline with people on short time. Local man Thomas Fryer, an enterprising entrepreneur, helped the waning economy, introducing his V for Victory Babies – jelly babies – and his V lozenges for a sore throat – both very popular. In 1890 Nelson was granted a Charter by Queen Victoria giving borough status. When the Labour party gained control of the council they put gas and water under their control long before Clement Attlee did it after WW2. In 1935 the Labour Council declined to pay for celebrations in the town for King George V's silver jubilee. They said they would rather spend on free dinners for school children and the jobless.

The financial crash in America in 1929 – known as the Wall Street Crash – affected British companies as well and the unemployment rate in Nelson, which had been only 6%, rose sharply to over 25%.

It wasn't the kind of place to spend a holiday. Jimmy Hogan, the legendary footballer who successful coached several European clubs, was born there. In Hungary he was looked on as the finest coach of his time. But there haven't been many famous cricketers emanating from the town, other than Learie. An exception was Australian fast bowler Edgar Arthur 'Ted' McDonald (1891–1937) who had successful years with Nelson CC between 1921–4. They wanted to keep him but he accepted a better offer from Lancashire and was granted a benefit after only five seasons. In his first season at Old Trafford he took a monumental 205 wickets. He had a short life, dying in a car crash near Bolton, aged forty-six.

James Manuel Blanckenberg, a South African medium pace bowler, preceded Learie. Today he would be looked on as a racist because at a testimonial game he refused to have a drink with the inoffensive black West Indian batsman George Headley, saying, 'I am a great admirer of your cricket but where I come from we don't fraternise with you fellows.' When he retired he went to live in Berlin and was believed to be a Nazi sympathiser. There was no record of when and where he died.

The Lancashire League was set up in 1892 with thirteen clubs and they had permission to sign two overseas players but in 1900 it was reduced to just one. In 2008 David 'Bumble' Lloyd, the England and Lancashire batsman who first made his name at one club, Accrington, gave an interview saying that the clubs should stop signing foreigners because they can't afford it. But the practice still carries on. The difference was that today they pay lower fees to young, aspiring overseas players instead of established Test stars.

Learie was back in Trinidad at the end of September and began his final season as an amateur in the Inter Colonial Tournament, representing Trinidad. Against a mainly Indian-descended British Guiana team he captured 9–96 and scored a swift 50, putting his side on the way to victory. Against the strong Barbados team he struck his first-class highest score of 133 out of Trinidad's 380. Three wickets and three smart catches saw Barbados bowled out for 108. Forced to follow on, he took four more wickets and Barbados managed just 109, losing by 163 runs. The Queens Park CC's committee awarded him a quarter of the gate receipts of the final match as a tribute to his genius.

He was now considered a celebrity and was invited to appear in a charity match in New York. He didn't quite reach the standard of his performances set out in the Big Apple newspapers – that he was the world's fastest bowler and the hardest hitter next to Gilbert Jessop – but he held a fantastic catch on the run and supporters rushed on to the field and shoved money into his pocket. He didn't hand any of it back, saying, 'There was nothing else to do but accept what the Gods had given me and a few minutes later I was bowling flat out with my pockets bulging and jangling.' He scored only five but routed the opposition with a blistering spell of 7–9.

Halfway through his spell a messenger came out to the middle and said, 'You've got to do something, boy. A demon bowler ought to knock the men about. The people are getting sort of restless.' Learie said he would try: he came roaring up to the crease to convince the uninitiated and knocked out a hapless batsmen, putting him down for the count. When the batsman was helped up he promptly retired.

The day before the match Norma accompanied him to a service in the St. Patrick's Cathedral and they were asked to move to the part where black people had to sit. It made them angry but they moved to avoid an embarrassing scene.

In September he was invited to appear in a West Indies side against Sir Julien Cahn's team at Jamaica. The 1st Baronet was the owner of a Nottinghamshire furniture company, which was later bought by the Great Universal Store company. A philanthropist, a lot of his wealth was spent taking high-class cricketers around the world to take on the locals. Not a very good cricketer himself, he usually picked himself in his side and fearing his shins might be injured, he pioneered batting pads which had to be blown up like a cycle tyre to make sure he wouldn't be hurt. He arranged 621 matches between 1929–39, losing only nineteen. Sir Julien's side included Test players – Lord Tennyson, Andy Sandham,

Ewart Astill, Stan Nichols and Nottinghamshire's William Wilfrid Whysall (1887–1930) who was another of that era who died early, a victim of septicaemia at the age of forty-three after tripping over and injuring an elbow on a dance floor.

Learie bowled well but his biggest contribution was to hold six catches in a high-scoring match at Sabina Park, which the Baronet's men won by 144 runs.

MCC (the England squad was still labelled that after the world's premier cricket club) brought an old, understrength side to the West Indies in 1929–30 with ten over thirty years old, and only five under that age. Walter Hammond, Harold Larwood and Maurice Tate wanted a winter's rest at home while another MCC England XI went to New Zealand. The party going to the Caribbean included Wilfred Rhodes who was fifty-two, George Gunn at fifty, and Patsy Hendren at forty. Still, even in those boiling hot days of incessant sunshine, the oldies managed a 1–1 draw.

The West Indies selectors recalled Learie from England where he was acclimatising ready for his debut in Nelson. He took eighteen wickets in the first three Tests and scored only one half-century before he missed the high-scoring draw in the final Test in Kingston where MCC sweated through 258.5 overs to reach 849 with Surrey's Andy Sandham (1890–1982) making the highest score of his career of 327. It was a Timeless Test occupying eight days. And it was certainly a good one to miss for Learie.

In the previous matches both sides peppered each other with bouncers, two years before the Bodyline series. Learie probably bowled most of them. Bob Wyatt said he bowled like lightning and from the start he bowled bouncer after bouncer at the batsman's head with only two fielders on the offside, somewhat an exaggeration one would think! Surprisingly, no one complained. Learie believed the short-pitched delivery was part of the armoury of a fast bowler. If anyone was hit he would be the first to rush up and offer apologies to the batsman. No one wore helmets and most batsmen of both sides were coached to keep their eyes on the ball and move away of the line of the oncoming missile so that an edged hook shot wouldn't strike them in the head.

The West Indies Board of Control – comprising only white people – handicapped their own side by giving the captaincy to four white men, one from each region, Barbados (Teddy Hoad), Trinidad (Nelson Betancourt), British Guiana (Maurice Fernandes) and Jamaica (Karl Nunes). They took turns to drop players from other regions and replaced them with their own selections. This ridiculous way of taking on other national teams lasted until the late 1950s when Sir Frank Worrell became the first permanent black captain.

George Alphonso Headley (1909–1983), aged twenty, born in Panama, made his debut in the First Test at Barbados and Learie advised him to 'play within your limitations. It's just another game.' George showed no sign of limitations, scoring 21 and 176. He was about to train as a dentist in Jamaica when he started to impress as the best batting talent in that part of the world. He was later acknowledged as the Black Bradman but his first nickname was Atlas because it was said he carried the rest of the team by his extraordinary number of runs. In those four Tests he made 703 runs, average 87.87. His first-class career stretched from 1927–54 and in his final Test made him the oldest West Indian player aged forty-four years and 236 days. In the 1939 tour to England he was the first West Indian Test player to score a hundred in each innings, at Lord's. Seventy-eight years later, Shai Hope did the same at Headingley in 2017. The Second World War interrupted Headley's chances of being the top West Indies batsman ever, restricting him to only twenty-two Tests. However, his batting average of 60.83 was phenomenal.

The dissension among the regions about the relative abilities of their players was typified by a section of the Barbados crowd on the first day of the Test when they booed Headley when he went in to bat in the first innings. They wanted one of the more experienced Barbados players, not a rookie. Coming in at first wicket down he was unfazed until the Essex slow bowler Jack O'Connor (1897–1977), who unusually bowled both off and leg breaks but no googlies, dismissed him by a slow delivery. Learie, a victim of his own impetuosity, made just 13 in the total of 369.

A feature of cricket in the 1920s was the number of bowlers used: England often had seven or sometimes more. When England replied with 467 the West Indies employed six with Learie having Andy Sandham lbw for 152. Learie's figures – 39–9–121–3 – were the best of the innings and the cricket writer of the *Barbados Advocate* wrote: 'There was only one player whose performance overshadows all others. That player was Learie Constantine. He outwitted Sandham, bowled Ames, took a good catch to dismiss Hendren and then mystified (*sic*) his spectators by taking two magnificent catches whereby O'Connor and Astill were returned to the pavilion. He is a wonder. This term admirably sums up his greatness.'

Learie won a bat for the best all-round performance despite scoring only 6 in the second innings of 384 and didn't take a wicket in the drawn match with England ending on 167–3. Lebrun was there supporting his son and former skipper Harold Austin, who made the presentations, said, 'there is no more charming and keen cricketer than Constantine senior, and as you see, ladies and gentlemen, the son has inherited the father's manners and keenness for the game. We enjoy watching you, Mr Constantine, as much as you enjoy your cricket.'

In those days, with the sun slowly setting on the British Empire, the cricket Boards would arrange collar and tie, blazered dinners after Tests and England's captain Calthorpe took the opportunity to criticise Learie's habit of bowling an excessive number of bouncers, in a non-controversial manner. He claimed that if Learie hadn't bowled short and aimed at the wicket he might have won the game for his side. 'There was no chance of a result while he bowled short with four short legs and two deep,' he said. A Dr L.C. Hutson had a long letter published in the *Advocate* saying that Larwood used these tactics in the previous year and so did Bill Voce (1909–1984) in the current series. Voce came from a coal-mining background, like Larwood, and his left over the wicket fast bowling was the ideal partner for him in the coming battles with Bradman and his aides.

Before the next Test at Port of Spain, Englishman Harry Mallett, the former Durham player who managed several West Indian tours, called Learie aside and asked him to cut out his intimidatory bowling. If he didn't, there would be unpleasantness and MCC's committee men wouldn't be happy. Learie happily agreed. He was never a Dennis Lillee or Jeff Thomson.

In the ensuing Test, Voce was the beneficiary. He still bowled his bouncers, but fewer in number, took 4–79 in 28 overs on the matting pitch and followed up with a match winning 7–70 in 37.2 overs in the second innings. Learie was one of his victims, having him caught after a run a minute 52 by Hendren and in the second innings the jokey George Gunn caught him for 16. In a warm-up game previously Gunn delighted the locals by advancing down the pitch against Learie's bowling and instead of trying to drive he played with a dead, defensive shot, time and time again. When it was Learie's turn to bat a high hit started to come down where Gunn, wearing an Indian-style *sola topee*, popular in the tropics, was standing. Gunn whipped his headwear off in his left hand and caught the ball in his right hand. The crowd roared with laughter. Pith helmets, as they are also known, are still used today in Vietnam.

Mallett was well respected in Caribbean cricket and almost a hundred years on the West Indian Board appointed another Englishman as CEO, Johnny Grave, the former Surrey executive who went on to serve as the commercial manager of the Professional Cricketers Association for seven years. His job was to oversee the West Indian Board's US40m budget and enlarge it. A tough job indeed!

Learie held nine catches in two previous games and told his colleagues, 'I've never fielded better.' But his luck suddenly changed in England's second innings of 425–8 when he dropped the stocky Elias Henry 'Patsy' Hendren, a cheery Cockney with Irish blood, early on. Hendren (1889–1962) went on to score 205 not out. 'Patsy' was a crowd-pleaser and in his thirty-year first-class career he hit 170 centuries. Betancourt used eight bowlers and once again, the willing Learie bowled most overs, forty with figures of 4–165. No West Indian reached 50 and the side stumbled to defeat by 167 runs.

An oddity was that the Nottinghamshire and England batsman Joe Hardstaff Senior (1882–1947) umpired in all four Tests. The cricketing bosses in the Caribbean didn't have much faith in their own umpires. He umpired in seventeen Tests in all and would have stood in more but for the fact that his son Joe Junior (1911–1990) turned out to be a regular for England in twenty-three Tests. There was a Joe Hardstaff cricketing dynasty because another Joe, son of Junior, played for Combined Services and later became secretary of Middlesex.

Learie's last Test appearance in the 1930 series took place at a ground built in 1884 named Bourda, which was hosting its first Test match. It soon turned out to be the flattest, easiest pitch to bat on anywhere. Several metres under sea level, it was surrounded by a moat and in its thirty Tests before a modern ground, Providence Stadium, was built outside Georgetown in 2005, several riots occurred, the worst in 1979 and 1999. An area called the Cornerstone in the Mound Stand was where the worst offenders took up their positions. The selectors, realising the local players were not up to international standard, only picked three Guyanese and normally that could have led to trouble.

One of the three, Maurius Pacheco 'Maurice' Fernandes (1897–1981) was appointed skipper in his second Test, won the toss, saw his side win their first ever Test by 289 runs and was dropped and never recalled. Trinidadian Clifford Archibald Roach (1904–1988) hit up his highest score, 209, and with England missing a number of catches and George Headley making a memorable 114, the West Indies finished on 471. Playing in such humid conditions Calthorpe's batsmen wilted and were fired out on a near-perfect pitch for 145 with Learie, 4–35, doing most of the damage. The touring party was distressed to be quartered in poor-standard accommodation and Learie had to share a bed with Headley. In that time, West Indians were used to it; England's veterans weren't.

Calthorpe could have made England follow on but his side batted a second time running up a target of 617. Headley's 112 in the total of 290 was of the highest standard. Learie's contribution was a duck. Wilf Rhodes, aged fifty-two, showed tremendous stamina in his forty overs in the first innings and another fifty-one in the second.

Hendren showed similar fortitude to top-score with 123 and Rhodes, blocking away for his slow motion 10 not out, almost snatched a draw. Last man Voce was bowled by Francis for two only fifteen minutes from time. Learie excelled himself again with remarkable figures of 40–17–87–5. His victims were quality batsmen – Sandham, Wyatt, Ames, Townsend and Astill – the last one trod on his wicket trying to avoid a bouncer.

There was a suggestion that he was unfit for the fourth and final Test. He was certainly extremely tired. But he was one of many talented West Indian cricketers who were victims of internal politics. Four new call-ups were two Jamaicans, a batsman Frank Martin and a leg break bowler Oscar Scott, and two Trinidadians, Sir Errol Santos, a medium pacer, and a slow bowler George Gladstone. Dos Santos, as he was known then, became Mr Big of West Indies cricket and was President of the Board for some years and he has a stand named after him in the Queen's Park ground. Twenty-nine players were used, almost double the usual number in winning sides.

As the series was tied, the captains agreed to play another game until a result was achieved – a timeless Test. Once England ploughed their way to 849 the chances of a West Indian victory evaporated and Headley's 223 led the revival in the second innings of 408–5. On the eighth day it rained and the skippers decided to call it off, enabling the England squad to catch their boat back home.

At the same time, Learie was on his way with his family about to start his second year with Nelson.

SIX

LANCASHIRE LEAGUE'S PHENOMENON

Tom Morgan, chairman of Nelson Cricket Club, and his committee had problems finding accommodation for Learie and Norma because of the colour of their skin. Hardly any black people had ever lived there. Finally they found a stern middle-aged woman who was prepared to take them in. She told them, 'No one else wanted you.' Just two rooms and a shared bathroom in Howard Street, opposite Whitefield School. Morgan and club captain Harold Hargreaves met them at Liverpool Docks near the end of April and they travelled back to Nelson with their luggage, which included his favourite bat.

The next day Learie noticed that children would jump up to the windows to catch a glimpse of these almost outer space intruders. He said, 'Curious people would walk up the road and look in the windows. They were laughing at us, not because we had black faces but because we were different from what they expected.' The unfriendly landlady was unsettled by these intrusions and soon after the Constantines moved a hundred yards away to rented rooms in Buccleuch Road.

They often talked about going home to Trinidad at the end of the first season, because of the weather and the unsociability of some of the inhabitants, some of whom left insulting letters and postcards in the letter box. He kept a letter postmarked Colne which started: 'Dear Nigger, if you start bumping them on Saturday you will get bumped, not half, so try to play the game and remember you are playing among white men and not niggers.' It took a few weeks before the abuse died down.

Learie raised the possibility of departing but Norma, usually the strongest partner in the relationship concerning family matters, said firmly, 'No, we are not going. We're going to stay. Let's stick it out.' Eventually they moved to rent a terraced house at 3, Meredith Street overlooking the town and lived there for almost twenty years. There is now an English Heritage Blue Plaque, placed close to the front door in 2011. The stone-built houses were constructed before the turn of the century on a steep hill and had originally four rooms. Now they have added another small bedroom and a bathroom. Behind the row of houses was another row of houses separated by a single lane, known as back-to-back houses in the north of England. At the rear was a small yard but no garden: no chance of young children playing with balls and bats.

I visited the house on November 10th in 2017 and from the outside it hasn't changed. Few people would see the Blue Plaque because the main road is situated twenty-five metres down the hill. A couple moved in a year previously and admitted they didn't know much about Learie. Jordie Cassidy and his partner Benjamin, a painter and decorator, have done a fine decorating job. They put up exquisite handmade plaques in the main room, after their children, six-year-old son Ben and their three-year-old daughter, with their birth dates. In the hall they have prominent boards on a wall saying 'Enjoy Your Life' and 'Love Life.' From the outside, the house looked like a typical mill town one, satanically stained by grime when the Industrial Revolution took over, but on the inside it gives the impression of happiness and contentment. There are thirteen narrow, dark steps to the first floor and luckily Learie, who drank only occasionally, never tripped over. The best feature was their front bedroom which overlooked the bowling green and in the distance, the Pendle Hills, which are famous for the three witch trials in the seventeenth century, which led to the start of the Quaker Movement.

Clearly, Learie and Norma were happy there. They had moved from a working-class to a middle-class area and they remained there until 1949 when he had stopped playing for Nelson. In his second season at Nelson, Gloria joined them and years later she recalled, 'Some people used to pass on the other side of the road when they saw him coming. He broke the barriers. They had been fed the idea black people were not really people, that they were less and were not very bright.'

Early on, he was invited to give out prizes at the Padham and District Sunday School cricket league in a packed cinema. A reporter from the *Nelson Leader* wrote: 'He performed his task splendidly and his speech of five or six minutes was a model of its kind. He spoke excellent English and was heard distinctly in a very large place.' Rev Wyatt of Burnley, the chief speaker, referred to Constantine not only as a cricketer but as a Christian gentleman and he said he followed his religion as much as he did his cricket. He couldn't say whether in his religion he had been successful but if the voice of the people was the voice of God, then in cricket he had been successful. It was a thoughtful, modest little speech that made a direct appeal to the audience, who were sorry he did not speak much longer. He had a word for all the prize-winners and in particular for a young boy who had won the prize for the neatest scorebook.

John Kay, the *Manchester Evening News* cricket correspondent, was the leading expert who had more knowledge about the Lancashire League than almost anyone in the county and he sometimes played alongside Learie in Nelson. I knew him, a nice man always willing to help colleagues. He said of Learie, 'He was the ideal League cricketer whose fast bowling was always a magnet for the crowd, his big hitting was an added attraction and also his superlative fielding. He dominated yet didn't obliterate. He encouraged the amateurs and praised them as fellow cricketers. Learie's sportsmanship was outstanding. He would always congratulate their opponents.

'He was assiduous of coaching children and a valued member of the local community as well as in every sense of the word a gentleman. No sick supporter ever lacked a pre-match word or even a hospital visit from him to provide the sort of medicine no doctor could better.'

The Nelson cricket ground Seedhill wasn't far away from Meredith Road. Many of the cotton mills which belched smoke had closed but the stubby chimney pots of the houses emitted an immense amount of smoke from coal fires. To brighten things up the club put up baskets of flowers in the front of the pavilion, which bore a resemblance to a pagoda. In 1982–3 it was replaced further to the north-east of the ground by a two-storey building which boasts a large function room with bars, office and kitchen. Upstairs there are a presidents' quarters, dressing rooms, the secretary's room and a tiny umpire's room. It cost a fortune and the money came from selling land to enable the construction of part of the M65 at the top of a steep slope. The deal was fixed by the council and it included a sports centre with a running track and a bowling green. The alterations made the cricket ground smaller and if Learie was alive he would have scored many more sixes, possibly putting some on the motorway.

It is ironic that the twenty-five-year-old professional in 2017 was a white first-class cricketer from Gauteng Province in South Africa named Devon Conway who has had his hopes of becoming a Test player dashed by the quota system used to ensure that more black cricketers are picked. He has now moved to New Zealand for two years to try to qualify to become a Kiwi.

A former secretary of the club Harold Standage said, 'Learie was a man of many talents on the cricket field and should he fail with either bat or ball, which of course he did from time to time, he was sure to electrify spectators in the field. Matches started at 2pm on Saturdays after the cotton mills closed at 11am. The cricket ground possessed large seated enclosures and a twin line of seats all round the ground. To ensure obtaining a seat, if the weather was reasonable, one had to be there by 12.30. Later arrivals had to stand for five hours. No grass ever grew on the terraces.'

Attendances went up and a match against Bacup drew an audience of 14,000, almost unprecedented. The average in Learie's stay was 8,000–10,000 and the extra income soon wiped away the club's debts. Previously the gates were counted in hundreds. Practice nets were held in midweek and would be watched by between 200 and 300 intent on seeing the new professional. Nowadays crowds watching first team fixtures are around 200 to 300. In 1929, Learie scored almost 1,000 runs for an average of 34 and took 88 wickets in 361 overs for an average of 12 in his first season, and that ensured he would stay on after his three-year contract. Nelson won the first six matches in 1929 with Learie picking up a sizeable amount of extra cash from a collection by making 87 against Bacup in his debut game. Inspired by his new star, they went on to win the championship by a canter.

His popularity with the other players, officials and supporters was reflected when he was asked to captain a Nelson touring side going to play in Scotland after the League programme finished. One of his ambitions was to see the beauty north of the border. Thirty-nine years later he was invited to become Rector of St. Andrews University. In his first touring game he scored 175 not out in Inverness and Nelson won the match by 271 runs. The *Scotsman* called his innings 'a display of hurricane hitting, putting the ball out of the ground three times and it included 29 fours.' Learie told the local Provost: 'No game helped the solidification of the Empire as much as cricket.' He was a fervent believer in that idea.

The next match was against Morayshire at Elgin, where I went to school in 1947–8, the winter of the big freeze, and Learie demolished the home side for 45 with figures of 7–15. In two more victorious games at Ayr, he took 6–46 at and 5–29. Later he often loved playing charity matches in Scotland where he helped to establish a regional sports council in the 1960s.

Lancashire people, in the main, are warm-hearted and Nelsonians soon took to the black family in their midst. Invitations for dinner were accepted and the Constantines became friends with a number of middle-class families who were still friends in later life. He had a habit of making a joke about himself. He would say, 'Who would come out worse when two people are walking towards each other in the dark, me or a white man?' and roar with laughter. In his book *Cricket and I* he told a story of a small boy whose parents were friends. 'On his first day at school he came home streaming with tears and crying out at me "Uncle Learie, you never told me you were coloured!"' The other boys had given him a hard time about it. Learie would coax him along, convincing him that people are all the same, irrespective of their colour. Over the years he kept in touch and both Learie and the boy took up jobs in the legal profession.

Harold Hargreaves, the cricket chairman, related an amusing story – 'Most of the houses at that time had large fireplaces and an oven all made of black cast iron and Friday was the popular day to clean and polish them with blackhead. I told the audience "Learie would be late because Mrs Constantine would be busy blackleading him ready for the weekend." He then arrived to be greeted with laughter. On being told what I had said, he grinned all over and turned the situation to his advantage.'

Learie was generally available to speak at local organisations, representing people from Trinidad and explaining that the sun in the Caribbean shone all day, with a few exceptions, whereas in Lancashire it was the other way, all rain and intermittent sun, like at Nelson. He spoke in a friendly way to everyone he encountered, especially people living below the breadline. The poverty reminded him of the poorer areas in Trinidad. Except his fellow Trinnies had the joy of breathing better air and eating more healthy food.

In 1966 he said, 'I must admit that being the first coloured professional cricketer who had come to the Lancashire League, I had a job to satisfy people that I was as human as they were.' At that stage he kept clear of local politics. Nelson was mainly ruled by Labour supporters, up against a few Conservatives and independents. He must have known Sydney Silverman, the MP for Nelson and Colne who was elected in 1935 and held the seat until 1968, and respected him. Silverman was a conscientious objector – refusing to be called up into the armed forces – and he was imprisoned on three occasions during the First World War and later campaigned, successfully, for the removal of capital punishment. A Jew, he also campaigned for the creation of a homeland for Jews in Palestine.

Learie joined the local library and started his legal studies and with spare time between matches he was keen on writing a book about his career. He broached the subject to his friend C.L.R. James and James had started writing a book himself entitled *The Black Jacobins.* In March 1932 James arrived in London and with hardly any money, stayed with the Constantines in Nelson. He had dabbled with writing reviews and about cricket in Trinidad without much reward and Learie encouraged him to go to England. As a staunch left-winger who by now was on his way to becoming a Marxist, he found himself in a hotbed of socialism in Lancashire.

He wanted Learie to join him in representing the views of West Indians now living in Britain through the League of Coloured Peoples set up in 1931. Learie, a man of sound principles and high moral standing, had to be careful about speaking out on issues of colour at the time. He thought it was too soon for him to sign up for another league, a political one. Eventually he did but James, one of the first to join, also joined the Independent Labour Party. Learie declined that one.

James wrote later: 'Within five weeks we had unearthed the politician in each other. Within five months we were supplementing each other in a working partnership which had West Indies self-government as its goal.' They were invited to attend meetings and the more confrontational approach by James won a lot of support. Learie had to tread more warily though.

His book entitled *Cricket and I* was published in 1933 and sales were moderately successful. He went on to write six more books, all written by himself – *Cricket in the Sun* and *Cricketers' Carnival*, both in 1948, *Cricketers' Cricket* in 1949, *Cricket Crackers* in 1950 and his most important work *Colour Bar* in 1954. In 1953 he collaborated with his friend Denzil Batchelor to write *Game of a Lifetime*. Hardly any famous cricketer has written so prolifically.

James was looked on as an intellectual and both men shared a passion for playing and dissecting cricket and putting it over in an acceptable way. Living in a town ruled by left-wingers, James's career thrived and he later attracted a lot of attention from his works. Learie paid for the publishing of his thirty-two-page pamphlet called 'The Case of West Indian Self-Government.' When *The Black Jacobins* was published it won critical acclaim and his *State Capitalism and World Revolution* followed after James moved back to London.

Learie knew Neville Cardus through writing about his exploits in the *Manchester Guardian* and persuaded the sports editor to give reporting work to James for the newspaper. The extra income enabled him to maintain himself and after a year living in Nelson, he was able to move out to a flat in Manchester, before finishing up living in London. The two men didn't see eye to eye on all subjects but both benefited from each other. James encouraged Learie to study for the Senior Cambridge Certificate to help his career outside of cricket. C.L.R.'s bestseller *Beyond a Boundary* came out in 1963 and is still selling today.

Learie was earning considerably more than almost all of the population in Nelson and agreed with the non-conformist ethic of sober living and thrift. He didn't smoke, rarely drank and didn't gamble, unlike most West Indian sportsmen. He spent his money sensibly but one extravagance was to buy a green Austin Seven with a chunk of his £500 summer's remuneration. He took his family to trips to the moors and other beauty spots. Young children wanted rides and Nelson's cricket chairman Tom Morgan, said, 'He would play cricket with them on the recreation ground and afterwards pack them into the Austin after matches and drive them around.'

Known as the 'Baby Austin' the vehicle was first brought out in 1922, and was a rare sight in Nelson. Hardly anyone could afford a car. The cramped four seats left little space to take luggage but with Norma often staying at home to look after Gloria when they arrived at the start of the 1930 season, a wet one, he was able to transport his gear. Norma wasn't a great cricket watcher. According to Gloria, 'she often sat in the car reading a book.'

Skipper Harold Hargreaves, a mill worker who used to start his work at 6am, was mainly self-educated and in his spare time he was an operatic conductor and composer. His opinion of Learie was: 'He was a good man and a simple one.'

John Kay of the *Manchester Evening News* described him as 'the perfect citizen.' Tom Morgan was one of his greatest admirers. He summed him up by saying, 'He never gave the club a moment's trouble during the whole of his association with us. We were living in the Depression and life was hard but he lifted our spirits.'

They weren't jealous of his newfound wealth. When Gloria was five she started at the Nelson Preparatory School whose headmistress was Miss Washington. She was the only black girl at the school until 1935 and at first, she was taunted about her colour. Learie told her not to bother about it, assuring her, 'We are among friends.' There was only one unsavoury incident, when another little child slapped her. She was said to have gone home in a flood of tears but Norma told her she shouldn't be a cry baby and if it happened again, she should fight back. Some time later there was another fracas and Gloria walloped the offender. No other child slapped Gloria again.

Between 1935 and 1939 Gloria attended the Convent of Our Lady of Lourdes in the neighbouring town of Colne and there was another incident when a boy spat in her face. The boy wasn't a pupil at the Convent and the matter was not pursued. All the girls wore short hair except Gloria because Norma insisted on plaiting her daughter's hair into four plaits. Gloria disliked plaits. The geography teacher drew Gloria's plaits on the board to illustrate the Nile delta, calling up Gloria before the class and pointed to her head, and the partings. Norma was upset about this and went to the school and protested to the nun in charge. The nun apologised. Years later, when the subject was brought up, she explained, 'It is easier to practise on someone else's head. Where have I found another child with hair like mine?'

During WW2 Gloria attended Nelson Grammar School, a co-educational school, and her fellow pupils elected her a prefect and a house captain. Her grades were of the highest standard and it wasn't a surprise when she returned to Trinidad years later and became the Head of St. Francois Girls' College (1964–1978). When she retired, she acted as an advisor in the Education Ministry of the Government.

In 1946 she was accepted at St. Andrew's University in Scotland where the Duke and Duchess of Cambridge were educated. Learie and Norma were immensely proud of her achievement. Hard work and determination helped her through.

Learie's cricketing career saw his wages being almost invariably topped up by 'nobbins' – collections from the crowd for scoring 50 or more, or five wickets or more at Nelson. Mill workers earned up to £100 a year and the unemployed, who were many, received a measly 75p in dole money each week. Sixpence was the admission to Nelson's matches and the club's weekly income totalled around £200. In the coming years his salary reached £750 a year and his bonuses and increments swelled the figure to over £1,000, making him one of the highest-paid sportsmen in the country. In 1934 he was offered £1,100 to join another club but he refused. The other thirteen League clubs benefitted handsomely from him appearing at their grounds and the combined extra income was said to be around £10,000.

Gloria emphasised his crowd-pulling attraction recounting a lovely story. 'When I was young I remember Dad was playing in a charity match and he was batting and thought he had a chance of being given out. He said to the umpire "That was close!" "Close," said the umpire, "you were out but people have paid good money to see you bat and they are going to see you bat."'

A correspondent in the *People* newspaper questioned the signing of Learie, saying, 'the effort to engage him, generally considered to be the best all-round cricketer in the world to play for Nelson has been the outstanding sensation of the season. Why do these Northern clubs require players of this calibre? How can they afford to pay these talented cricketers and pay their return fare to the other side of the world? Edward Ashton, club secretary, was reported saying "exceptional cricketers with magnetic personalities are essential to League cricket. The public will not flock to see amateurs alone." Mr Ashton would not disclose the precise terms that had been agreed but confirmed that, in addition to paying Constantine's passage to and from Trinidad, the professional was to receive the most liberal consideration ever paid, a factor which helped to persuade the great man to sign was the fact that he would win £1 for 50 runs or five wickets taken plus a collection from the spectators.'

Seven matches were lost by rain in the 1930 season and Bacup managed to wrestle the championship off Nelson. On August 16th, Haslingden scored 169 and Nelson's openers were proceeding cautiously without taking risks and Learie said to his skipper Harold Hargreaves – an outstanding all-rounder – 'put me in when the first wicket falls.' Hargreaves had put his own name down as three but realising Nelson might not qualify for a scoring rate bonus, he said, 'All right but make sure you play yourself in first.' Learie strode out to the wicket with cheers and waves from a near capacity crowd, and his first four deliveries went for 2, 4, 2 and 4. He continued scoring at a fast rate and his 90* was the main reason Nelson won by seven wickets. When he came in the pavilion, expecting a reprimand for disobeying his orders, he told Hargreaves, 'Now, Harold, if I played my cricket like some professionals play theirs, I should be paid the same as them. As I play my cricket to entertain, I draw two or three times as much as them and we get gate receipts in proportion." Hargreaves had to agree.

There was a certain degree of boastfulness in his remark and this drew criticism. Another frank opinion about 'boring' Roses matches flared into a nationwide controversy which embarrassed him. He was invited to play in an evening game against a Stockton and District XI in Stockton and made only seven runs in three balls before losing his wicket. He was interviewed by a reporter named Larry Semmens from the *Northern Echo*, who asked him what he thought of the bi-annual encounters between Yorkshire and Lancashire. In the next day's *Echo* there appeared a rather long, critical article on the way these matches were conducted. 'They usually take six or seven hours for 200 runs and it is a wash out', it said. 'You get an orthodox batsman playing against orthodox bowlers to orthodox fields and little happens. If a batsman is hitting about the field and the bowler is keen to get rid of him, while fielders are expectant of the ball that will be hit their way, everyone enjoys it. Why pat a half volley because a man is on the boundary?

'In England the batsmen take so long to get their eye in. I also get my eye in but I don't forget to hit the loose balls. The key to the matter is the batsman, whether he shall be lively, or dull. In our tour of England in 1928 the West Indies side was all out for under 200. This meant the match must finish which is much better than the "no boundaries before lunch" philosophy.'

The article was given a double spread and the contents were wired to the national press. The Rose counties, particularly Lancashire, took exception and some officials were incensed. Some time later when the subject of him becoming a member of Lancashire was broached, they were violently opposed. Unused to dealing with news reporters as distinct to cricket writers, he insisted that his views were taken out of context.

The cricket between the rivals of Yorkshire and Lancashire was invariably dour with neither side conceding and it often still happens today. It goes back to The Wars of the Roses which lasted between 1455 and 1487. Eighteen bloody battles were fought all over England and thousands of nobility, retainers and mercenaries were slaughtered. Finally Henry Tudor's Red Rose army defeated the White Rose one of Richard III at Bosworth. Then Henry married Elizabeth of York, the eldest daughter of Edward VI, and he insisted the two Houses were now united. His claims were still disputed but he went ahead to crown himself as Henry VII.

So much skulduggery took place – two princes were mysteriously murdered in the Tower of London and various claimants to the throne were illegitimate – that Shakespeare wrote about it in his plays. Today's school children learn the facts and it surfaced again when the bones of Richard III were discovered beneath a car park in Leicester in 2012. Four years later the bones were reinterred in a hideous rectangular casket in Leicester Cathedral.

Learie relished League cricket because he was almost always fresh and ready to give his maximum on Saturdays, unlike most of the county players. As rain started, however light, they were telling the umpires to bring them in – it was too dangerous. The philosophy in the League was to stay out as long as possible and not worry about a shower or two.

In one of his seven books he defended himself eloquently against criticism which suggested that playing in Lancashire League was a soft option compared to county, state or international cricket. 'Many times I have been criticised more in sorrow than in anger for going into League cricket at all,' he said. 'I'll read that I threw away my abilities and elected to join a game with technical inferiors in cricket skill. I only wish my critics had to face some of the batsmen and bowlers I met there and to try and retrieve some of the situations with which I was faced. I resent the implication that I was taking things easy. To anyone who has watched a needle game the innuendo is ludicrous enough. Never in my life have I played harder than in Lancashire.'

He was right. Some of the greatest cricketers of all time played for League clubs in the 1930s – George Headley from the West Indies, Amar Singh of India, Bill Merritt of New Zealand, home-grown Sydney Barnes, Fred Root, Cecil Parkin and many more, backed by skilled amateurs whose knowledge of the game was handed down by the previous generations. They were all competitive and sledging was the norm. To succeed, they had to be mentally hardened cricketers. When Learie left Nelson at the end of his 1937 season he was succeeded by Lala Amarnath (1911–2000), the father of Indian Test cricket who scored the first century of the Indian side in Tests. He went on to captain India and his all-round feats were exceptional. One oddity about his bowling was that he took only four paces to deliver his wickedly in-swinging medium deliveries.

Nelson signed him despite the fact that he was sent home for alleged undisciplined behaviour during the tour of England in 1936. India's captain was the eccentric Maharajkumar of Vizianagram, known as 'Vizzy' who was definitely the worst ever captain of India, probably the worst in the history of the game. Amarnath soon pointed out his failings and though he was the outstanding all-round player in the party, he found himself on the first boat leaving to Mumbai.

After WW2 Nelson signed a lesser-known player named Albert Nutter in 1945, followed by big names like Ray Lindwall, Johnny Wardle, Neil Hawke, Sarfraz Nawaz, Collis King, Larry Gomes, Kapil Dev, Steve Waugh, Craig McMullan and others.

One of Learie's finest innings – he claimed it himself – was his 98 before he was caught and bowled by Sydney Barnes when Nelson was struggling. He came in at 68–3 and was 45 not out with the total 118–9 but he took the total to 175. Barnes restricted Learie to a very small proportion of his deliveries from the great bowler. And his field was cannily set, blocking most of his attempted shots. But Learie was able to turn a probable defeat into a triumph.

Learie contributed 801 runs and took ninety-one wickets at 8.15 apiece that year. Nelson did the double, winning the Worsley Cup as well. The tournament was unique. The batting side had to suspend their innings at 130 and if the other side reached 130, they would bat a second time. His fearsome bowling made sure the opposition didn't bat twice.

Only one West Indian bowler consistently came up with similar figures in the Lancashire League – Charlie Griffith when he played for Burnley and Lowerhouse in the 1960s. In a four-day period Learie had shattering figures of 8–21 against East Lancashire and 8–24 against Rawtensall.

His nadir at Nelson was reached when he made 1,000 runs, a club record, in 1933 when he recorded three hundreds and seven fifties with no ducks. Forty-four years later another Trinidadian, Hilary Angelo 'Larry' Gomes, the left-hand batsman who played in sixty Tests, beat his record. Learie also took 96 wickets. Supremely fit, he only missed two more matches to play for the West Indies, otherwise he would have done the double. Gomes was more of an accumulator, like Shrivnarine Chanderpaul, and didn't have the appeal of a Constantine.

A knee problem – pounding down his left foot on the batting crease – slowed him down with a sore cartilage in 1934. He had to keep going because he had been granted a benefit. Other grateful League clubs had a whip-round and contributed £250 to his fund. Some club officials pointed out that there is no mention in the League rules to give a benefit for only five seasons' work. They were overruled. Rochdale of the Central Lancashire League made him a huge offer, dwarfing his Nelson's contract, and he didn't want to uproot his family. The extra money from his benefit was another factor in making his decision.

William Barlow, the League secretary, said, 'The sum of £250 was not too great to show that the other clubs were grateful for the financial benefit conferred upon them by the remarkable drawing power of the most attractive professional the League has ever seen.' Previously, Accrington had consulted Learie about signing Don Bradman after the two men became friends on the West Indies tour to Australia in 1930–1 and they made a League record offer to Bradman, who was twenty-two at the time. After several weeks of dithering, Bradman finally cabled the club and apologised, saying he was no longer available. In his brief cable he thanked the club for 'having pleasant negotiations with me.' Instead they signed up all-rounder Alan Fairfax (1906–1955) whose speciality was hooking. Fairfax made three centuries and the quickest one was at the expense of Learie who by this time was troubled by his knee. Wounded in the First World War, Fairfax ran a cricket school in London before he was forced to retire. He died at the age of forty-eight.

Learie's career-best bowling performance was when he obliterated Accrington for 12 at Seedhill on May 11. Accrington had been his debut appearance when he arrived in 1929 and he disappointed the crowd by being outdone by his colleagues. This time he wanted to put on a display. In thirty-seven balls he took 10–10, setting a League record. Eight batsmen were bowled, seven for ducks. The top scorer was Will McDonough with four. His family still have the ball which he used, mounted and displayed in their house in Point Cumans, overlooking the Caribbean sea.

At the end of the season a specialist advised Learie to have the cartilage out. A lot of sportsmen in that era had similar operations and never played again but Learie was one of the lucky ones. The surgery was undertaken in a Liverpool medical centre and within six weeks he ditched his crutches and did a lot of brisk walking up and down the hills of Nelson. All the exercising he had done over the years proved the answer to staying fully fit.

After the season ended he received an invitation from the Nawab of Moin-ud-Dowlah, whom he hadn't met before, to coach in Hyderabad. He accepted with alacrity especially as the long journey via the Suez Canal by steamer gave him time to rest in the sun and improve the condition of his knee. His arrival was an eye-opener. He had lived in both Trinidad and Nelson and saw the extreme poverty of the majority of the two populations but he was deeply shocked at the inequality existing in India. Barefoot people wearing rags lived on the packed, smelly streets, asking for money. Some cut off an arm to attract the attention of others who looked wealthy. Not many handed over cash though. It was almost impossible to avoid the beggars. Better-attired men and women wanted his autograph with their incessant cries of 'Please sir, just one, please sign.' Most times he would sign.

He stayed in the Maharajah's palace and said, 'I was given a suite of rooms and to describe the place would be to recount the marvels of the Arabian nights, gold couches, gold chairs, gold implements of every sort.' He was driven around in Rolls-Royces but driving wasn't a pleasant experience because of the mayhem on the roads thronged by tuk-tuks, bicycles, ancient Ambassador taxis, cattle, monkeys and pedestrians, all making excessive noise and polluting the already polluted atmosphere. For all that, it is a fascinating place, as Learie found.

The Maharajahs vied with each other to try and invite big-name cricketers and in the 1930s Jack Hobbs, Herbert Sutcliffe, George Hirst, Jack Hearne, Roy Kilner, Abe Waddington, Maurice Leyland, Wilfred Rhodes and Harold Larwood among others made the trip. Most of them were Yorkies but after WW2 the great Fred Trueman declined and Geoffrey Boycott, who went on the tour with England in 1981, was sent home by Raman Subba Row, the tour manager, for playing golf when he was ill during a Test match in Eden Gardens, India's biggest cricket stadium.

Health and safety were words hardly used in India in those days. The incidence of accidents on overloaded, potholed roads and the upset of stomachs caused by polluted water meant that hardly anyone from abroad escaped those two evils. Despite having more wealth than most countries, India still hasn't solved the problem of poor infrastructure.

Most cricketers suffer severe diarrhoea and sickness and Boycott was struck down in that Test. His excuse was that he wanted to get away from the hubbub and breathe some fresh air on a golf course. Whether Learie caught the bug is questionable. His batting failed to match the standards of the best Indian batsmen and his bowling was affected by the extreme heat. But the money was good.

One of the most dramatic matches Learie took part in was on the Silver Jubilee Day in 1935 when he was opposed to another Indian all-star Ladhabhai Nakum Amar Singh (1910–1940), an all-rounder whose medium-fast swing bowling was described by Wally Hammond: 'he came off the pitch like a crack of doom.' The phrase probably came from his ghostwriter. Len Hutton had problems handling his bowling in Tests and reckoned he would be a contender for the World XI.

Amar Singh was Colne's first professional and a capacity of 14,000 men and boys, and a few ladies, were in their places well before the start. Colne batted first and Learie was, unusually, the least effective bowler as their batsmen toiled to make 164 on a typical up and down pitch. It was a local derby – Colne was just two miles away – and the excitement mounted when Nelson's batsmen came and went against the sizzling deliveries from Amar Singh. His action, off a comparatively short run, exploded into frenzy as he let the ball go with immaculately straight bowling which burst into late swing. He was almost unplayable and Learie was the only batsman to withstand it. Eventually he made a half-century and qualified for a bounteous collection.

When the last pair took the scores level there was frenzy, too, around the ground with almost everyone on their feet. Alf Pollard was facing and in came Amar Singh with another yorker aimed at the middle stump. There was a collective roar from him and his fielders as they screamed 'Howzat!' and the umpire's first finger went up. Match tied with Amar finishing with 9–61. He was yet another cricketer whose life was cruelly cut short: in 1940 he died from pneumonia at the age of thirty.

Nelson made it a hat-trick of championship titles in 1936, helped by a lesser total of runs from Learie, 632, but his eighty-six wickets were a clincher. During the winter he spoke often to Norma over the weeks about his future. He already had taken a part-time job with a Nelson solicitor, run by a teammate Alec Bertwell, and was aiming to qualify as a barrister when it was time to move to London. He was thirty-five and his reactions, especially in the field, had slowed down.

He decided he would have his ninth and final summer with Nelson and then depart. No professional had lasted so long in one club, and won the hearts of the populace. It was an amicable meeting with the committee and they understood and thanked him profusely for what he had done – upgraded Nelson to almost first class. Nelson, and Learie, were known throughout the land.

There was just one peak left for him to aim at – recording his highest score, making the highest individual score ever in the League. The match was against East Lancashire CC in Blackburn on a bank holiday in 1937. The pitch was flat and easy-paced and Nelson won the toss and batted. Some strange things happened: firstly a stocky New Zealander from Canterbury opened the bowling with variable leg breaks and googlies. He was named Bill Merritt (1908–1977) and his Test career was up and down, like his bowling. He was the club's professional.

Nine Nelson batsmen were all bamboozled out by Merritt, except Learie, who came in at four. His power play lifted the innings to 141–8 when Harold Hargreaves emerged and proceeded to have a tactical discussion. 'I'll count the balls and make sure you score off the last ball of every over,' Hargreaves said. 'It worked admirably and fours and sixes flashed from Learie's bat and, at one time, there were three balls in use, two on the field and one in play. I was eventually out for 10 at 262–9.

'Learie realised the last over was being bowled prior to a declaration – his score was 192 – when he danced down the pitch in a fairly obvious attempt to let Merritt finish with the ten wickets, but it wasn't to be. For one reason or another, the bails were not removed and a declaration was made with the score of 284–9.' Learie, eight short of a double-century, tried to sacrifice himself to allow Merritt to claim a first-ever ten-wicket haul. Not many cricketers would have done that. He batted for just under two hours and hit five sixes and twenty-seven fours. He was dropped on one.

Merritt's figures were 24–2–136–9. I played against him twenty years later in a friendly match at Ventnor CC, the ground in the Isle of Wight which has the steepest cricketing slope in the UK and is known appropriately as Steephill Hill. He was nearly fifty but he was still bamboozling batsmen. An Anglophile, he played rugby league for Wigan and Halifax, and ran a business in Dudley before retiring to Canterbury. Wally Hammond – or was it his ghostwriter? – said of one of his mystery balls, 'It was like a cobra, one of the nastiest balls I ever had to deal with.'

In 1937 Learie told the committee of Nelson CC he wanted to leave at the end of the season, ending his nine tumultuous years with them. The Mayor wanted to start a petition asking him to stay and Learie was adamant: he couldn't change his mind. At some matches the town band played 'Abide With Me' and people in the street pleaded for him to remain. Morgan issued a statement saying, 'Constantine is not leaving us on any question of terms. We are sorry to lose him. There is no other cricketer in the world who combines all the qualities that Constantine possesses.' Years later Learie wrote: 'If I had not come; if I had stayed in Trinidad, I could not have been the person I am today. I am a better person for coming. I am better materially. I am better socially. I have grown more tolerant. I am a better citizen for the time I spent in Nelson.'

That summer the runs and wickets poured out and Nelson won their fourth championship, a record. His record for nine years' work was matches 225, runs 6,550, highest total 192*, average 37.21, wickets 299, average 9.90, best bowling 10-10, catches 133. Entertainment 10 out of 10.

Rochdale, the Central Lancashire League, repeated their offer of a contract similar to Nelson's in 1939. His brother Elias (1912–2003) was playing with Rochdale and that was one of the reasons he chose Rochdale. Learie earned £812 for twenty weeks' work there and his final year proved to be something of an anticlimax. One of the highlights was at a gathering of friends when Learie and Elias resurrected their childhood habit of throwing crockery at each other and catching the items. 'That's how we learned how to catch the ball, you couldn't dare drop them,' said Learie with a chuckle.

Rochdale was only fifteen miles from Nelson and they remained in their Meredith Street house. He was given the Freedom of Nelson in 1963 and in 2011 the local council put up his Blue Plaque, and sadly it is hardly seen. But many of the 29,135 people of Nelson will never forget him.

SEVEN

LEARIE TAKES LICKS FROM THE BAT OF DON BRADMAN

Charlie Macartney was the man who brought about the first-ever West Indies tour to Australia in 1930–1. It was one of Learie's major objectives, touring Down Under, and taking on the great Don Bradman. He managed to dismiss Bradman once in the five Test series but only after Bradman had scored 223 in the Third Test at the Exhibition Ground in Brisbane. Bradman followed up with 152 in the Fourth Test at Melbourne.

Unlike today, there were warm-up games before Tests and he succeeded in bowling Bradman for 10 against the New South Wales team at Sydney. He wrote, triumphantly, describing the six wickets he took at a cost of 24 runs, all bowled, 'the ball was slower so as to bring Don out to make his pet stroke, steering the ball through the slips. He does so before realising that there is a devil in it, and his off stump goes for a walk.'

Macartney used his persuasive charm to talk the Australian Board into agreeing to allow a nearly all-black team into an almost all-white country which had tough restrictions on migrants. Most of the states in Australia drew up restrictive laws and in 1930 the government cancelled financial benefits for immigrants, even from Europe. But with the population falling they changed their minds five years later and allowed in people who had trades and professional jobs from their own country. After WW2 the government launched a 'populate or perish' policy and the population shot up to 23m. Words like 'Poms' and 'Wogs' were replaced by 'New Australians.' 'Poms' remained in common use – especially on cricket fields – and it derived from Prisoners of Mother England, those who were forcibly transported to Australia in the seventeenth and eighteenth centuries.

Learie was assured by Macartney that there wouldn't be a problem about a West Indies cricket team arriving and Bradman supported the idea. The two cricketing champions had great respect for each other and Bradman said of Learie: 'he was the best West Indian bowler and without hesitation I rank him the greatest fieldsman I have ever seen.' He was less effusive about his batting: too much bravura and not enough common sense about building an innings which could win matches.

Several West Indians, like the legendary George Challenor, were past their best by 1930 and no one gave the squad any chance of winning. Macartney thought they might beat New Zealand but certainly not Australia. None believed that George Copeland Grant (1907–1978), known as Jackie, should be captain. He was chosen only because he was white. He'd never captained a first-class team when he was given the honour. Born in Port of Spain of wealthy parents, he won Blues in football and cricket at Cambridge University. A cheery, plucky right-hand batsman, he made some extraordinary catches in the gully and by the end of the series he had earned a lot of praise for his leadership against the odds.

Grant's uplifting personality soon won the confidence of his players. As an amateur, he qualified for a captain's expenses while the others were paid a flat £300 for the three-month tour.

The sea journey from the Caribbean via the Panama Canal lasted a month and the ship docked at Wellington to drop off supplies and enabled the tourists to take part in a practice match against a New Zealand XI. The Windy City lived up to its name and the match was wrecked by storms. But there was enough time for Learie to dismiss six young, petrified batsmen at a cost of 24 runs.

The reception the polyglot West Indian squad – from Trinidad, Jamaica, Barbados and British Guiana – received at Sydney eased their fears about race. They were treated as equals, not underlings, and with enthusiasm. Most of them had British passports and there were no weighty forms to be filled in. The Australians wanted to see them in action, particularly Learie and George Headley. A writer from the Australian Cricketer said of Learie: 'he looks like a panther, a brilliant player capable of doing anything in any department. He appears to be a law unto himself in the field. He had the strongest personality of any cricketer that has ever visited Australia.' There were five Test matches and seven matches against State sides, a hefty requirement that needed an immense amount of rail travel.

After two days of practice, they took on the Sheffield Shield champions New South Wales at the Sydney Cricket Ground. Built on a rubbish dump, the ground staged the first Test match in 1882, and three years after a riot took place. There are a record number of eleven statues of eminent cricketers around the ground, more than the whole of the Test match grounds in England. Bradman, naturally, was later honoured but in 1930 he was in trouble after being docked £150 good-conduct bonus for breaching the rules about publishing a book without permission. He had just set a record with his 334 at Headingley and a publisher wanted to bring out a book.

On the second day of the NSW match a crowd of 29,000 turned up to see him bat. His reputation of being an independent spirit was enhanced, not damaged by his rows with the Board. The spectators weren't concerned about his so-called selfishness and being aloof. All they wanted was to see him batting through the day. He nearly did before he was out for 73. Learie ruffled him with his 85mph bowling, much of it pitched short, but he failed to take his wicket in both innings. In Bradman's second innings he made just 22.

The first round between the two champions went to Learie, whose 6–45 in eleven eight-ball overs might have been an indication that the series wouldn't be a walkover. With the bat, he slammed 59 runs in thirty-five minutes and Monty Noble, one of Australia's heroes, said of his all-round talents: 'he is certainly unique in everything.' Losing by only four wickets, Grant's players considered it as a moral victory. A total of 56,454 saw the four day's play and the receipts, for only a friendly not a Test, brought in a huge sum of £3,488.

The West Indians cricketers of 1930 were novices when it came to the science of cricket. Whereas the Australians kept records and indexes of information about the strengths and weaknesses of their opponents, the tourists played it by ear. Their natural talent went a long way but when it fell short, they had no intricate plans to help each other. The result was chaos, with the first four Tests being overwhelmingly won by the Australians. In three Tests Australia only batted once in each, winning by an innings each time. And their batting line-up was reckoned to be one of the strongest ever put out – Bill Ponsford (1900–1991) was one of the first to use a heavy bat, known as Big Bertha; he averaged 48.22 in Tests; Archie Jackson (1909–1933) born in Rutherglen, Scotland, who died of tuberculosis at the age of twenty-three, averaged 47.20; the peerless Don Bradman (1908–2001) with the best average of all, 99.94; Alan Falconer Kippax (1897–1972), the arch stylist, average 36.12; Stan McCabe (1910–1968), average 48.21; skipper Bill Woodfull (1897–1965), average 46.00, who had four nicknames: The Unbowlable, Rock of Gibraltar, Wormkiller and Old Steadfast; and Alan Fairfax (1906–1955), average 51.25.

Another factor was the unorthodox bowling of Clarrie Grimmett (1891–1980), the gnome-like, bald leg break and googly bowler who introduced the flipper, the one that went straight on with backspin to fool the batsmen with its slower pace. He made his Test debut at thirty-four and averaged six wickets per game and was first to reach 200 wickets. Born in Dunedin, he made his name in Sydney as a sports writer after being a signwriter and bowled with a round arm delivery which fooled a generation of top batsmen. Neville Cardus said of him: 'he was the master of the surreptitious arts.' Grimmett took thirty-three wickets in the West Indies series and not even Learie collared his tantalising bowling.

In the First Test in Adelaide, Learie came in at five and was dismissed by Grimmett for 1 and 14 with Australia winning by ten wickets. Despite his age – he had just turned forty – 'Scarlet' (for the Pimpernel) Grimmett bowled forty-eight overs, nineteen of them maidens and took 7–87. Learie only managed one wicket for 116 runs and it was a chastening time for him. Even Bradman claimed a wicket – for just 15 runs.

Against poor opposition in Tasmania, Learie came in at 122–4 and provided a another large crowd with a fire-cracking 100 in just fifty-two minutes. The West Indians went on to win by an innings and 50 runs, their first victory on Australian soil. They celebrated Christmas after the close of play in a second match, which was curtailed by rain. The journey back by a ferry from Launceston to Sydney for the Second Test was interminable – much of the 589 miles spent bumping up and down on fierce waves.

Whether their stomachs were still in turmoil on January 3rd, the third day of the Sydney Test, one didn't know but it could have been an excuse. Facing Australia's 369, of which Ponsford accounted for 183 runs, they were hustled out for 107. Grimmett, with 4–54, was again the key bowler. Thomas Welbourne Wall (1904–1981), known as Tim, was reckoned to be the fastest and the premier bowler in the Southern Hemisphere in the 1930s but he was dropped. The selectors brought in another veteran, the forty-eight-year-old Herbert Ironmonger (1882–1971) who was known as 'Dainty' because of his unwieldy bulk. He bowled left arm medium pace with a wicked leg break, which gave an extra twirl, through having had the top joint of the forefinger accidentally cut off in a sawmill. He also bowled the Chinaman, the one that came from the off. The Australian critics rated him as their country's worst-ever fielder.

These two 'mystery' bowlers created havoc on the final day, shooting out Grant's baffled batsmen for 90. It was a crushing win for the Aussies by an innings and 172 runs. The Australian Board members were wondering whether they had made a mistake to invite the West Indies. Receipts had dropped so much that they were losing money.

Bradman soon dissipated any fears about the attendance at the Exhibition Ground in Brisbane when he piled up 223 in the Third Test before mis-hooking a short ball from Learie and was caught by Grant off a skier at square leg. A large crowd was disappointed not to see him beat the highest Test score of Worcestershire's Reginald Erskine 'Tip' Foster (1978–1914) – 287 at Sydney in 1903. One of seven brothers – all educated at Malvern College, costing their father a huge amount of money – he was the only sportsman who captained England both in cricket and football. He worked in the Stock Exchange in the winter and was one of the outstanding sportsmen of his time. Sadly he died at the age of thirty-six in 1914 through diabetes. Ten years later he might have been saved: two Canadians came up with an effective cure for the disease.

Learie may well have got rid of Bradman early on. A fast out-swinger came off the outside edge of his lightweight bat and flew to the fielder at first slip who was unable to hold on to it. Learie had both Ponsford, who made 109, and Kippax, with 84, dropped as well. He and his quick bowlers soon tired in the 35°C heat as Australia reached an unassailable 558.

George Headley had made only 27 runs in the two Tests but now he showed his class and determination. His patient 102* in the West Indies' first innings of 193 was not enough to avoid another follow-on. This time he failed in the second innings, only posting a top score 28 out of a total of 148. The weather was excruciatingly hot, stoked up by heat from a volcano drifting over across the South Pacific Sea from New Zealand. The Australians were making a habit out of follow-ons. They were victorious by an innings of 217 runs.

Before the Brisbane Test, Learie was opposed by Australia's first Aboriginal cricketer Eddie Gilbert (1908–1978) in a warm-up match against Queensland. Under the regulations he had to get written permission for travelling from his Aboriginal settlement to another state. Many Australians believed he was faster than Learie and his colleagues and was more dangerous with his bouncers. He stood just five feet eight inches and weighed only nine stone. He bowled off five paces, with or without boots. Just before the Test he bowled Bradman for a duck and later Bradman claimed Gilbert was the quickest bowler he'd played against.

Gilbert had trouble to keep his right arm fully straight and he was no-balled on several occasions. He experimented with a piece of wood strapped on his bowling arm but wasn't able to cure the fault. Learie had an outstanding match; he scored 75 in under an hour, dismissed seven batsmen and caught three catches. His anticipated century in his second innings was ruined when his rocket shot bounced off the bowler's hand into the grasping hands of mid-off who was not able to hold on to it. Another fielder dived and caught the rebound before it hit the ground. As he trudged off, Learie said, 'I went into the pavilion a sad, injured man.'

Gilbert had a successful match, taking 5–65 and 2-26. He also hit Learie with a six over fine leg. A lingering shoulder injury restricted him to just 224 runs and 87 wickets in his brief first-class career. Eighty-seven, of course, is the Australian bad luck sign.

Learie made a habit of mashing the weaker sides before taking on South Australia in Adelaide. Against the NSW Country Districts in Newcastle he hit six sixes in his 147 in ninety-three minutes and his bowling analysis was 9–77. Next, he opened against a Geelong XI, made 20 from the opening over and was out for 80 well before sitting down for lunch. A seventeen-year-old Lindsay Hassett (1913–1993) caused a shock when he too made 147 and forced the tourists to follow on.

One of nine children, the poker-faced, diminutive Hassett went on to succeed Bradman as Australia's captain. A decent man with a wonderful sense of humour, he once tethered a goat to a bed where Bradman was sleeping and on another occasion, he jumped into the bed in a hotel where Jim Swanton was sleeping. A Catholic, he discouraged sledging opponents on the field when he became captain.

Bradman wasn't a sledger either but the ethos of insulting opponents still happens when the Australians play the game. Not having met Bradman and knowing that he always answered letters – except toxic ones – I wrote to him asking if he could write a message for brochures for tours by English schools going to Australia. For the first one he typed out 500 words and ended with this sage advice: 'We live in a world where we are short of leaders and my advice to youngsters is to keep a diary. They might become successful leaders and if they keep a diary they will be able to write their memoirs, to inspire those who follow.' The second instance he had just passed ninety and sent a letter saying he was recovering from a stroke and apologised for not being able to write another article. His writing was shaky. In every sense, he was a great human being.

Learie strained a leg muscle before the Fourth Test in the cavernous MCG known as 'The Shrine' in Melbourne but recovered enough to take part. Perhaps he shouldn't have bothered because it ended in just two days, with the Windies losing by an innings and 172 runs. It was another scorching day, the pitch was hard and bouncy and Grant made the right decision to bat because rain was forecast on the second day. Thirty-nine of the fifty overs needed to bowl out the visitors for 90 were sent down by Ironmonger – 20–7–23–7 – and Grimmett – 19–7–46–2. This pair's average age was 45. There were five ducks and only Headley, perfecting his defensive technique, lasted three hours for a best score of 33.

Some West Indian batsmen have had historical weaknesses against 'mystery' spin bowlers. Most of their cricket is played on hard, bouncy pitches and they relish those conditions. Slow, low pitches with the pace taken off the ball – up against bowlers like Shane Warne and Muttiah Muralitharan – are anathema to them. In the *Wisden Almanack* list of the thirty best Test bowlers there is only one West Indian slow bowler mentioned – Lance Gibbs, the off-spinner placed at twenty-nine with 309 Test wickets. He was a really an orthodox off-spinner with long fingers which gave the ball a tremendous twirl on flat pitches.

Only 3,969 spectators paid for their tickets and the Australian Board met to consider reducing the prices for the second day. Woodfull and Ponsford opened and it became a different game – they roared along like a couple of speeding Holden cars, the fastest vehicle of the age. Ponsford was unluckily stumped for 24 when the ball came back off the pads of wicketkeeper Barrow, but Bradman 92* and Woodfull 75* came in when rain ended the first day's play with a lead of a hundred. Realising Bradman might have a chance to beat Foster's world Test record, the officials cancelled plans to cut ticket prices.

Rain fell overnight and with no covering of the pitch, conditions deteriorated. It became a sticky dog pitch with the ball jumping off a length. Woodfull was run out for 83 – it was Bradman's fault – Archie Jackson fell to Learie for 15 and Stan McCabe was also run out, for two. Bradman was dropped at 92 and toiled to 152 before he was caught at long off, which included two fives. Woodfull declared on 328–8.

Learie was asked to open in a vain bid to knock out Grimmett and Ironmonger off their length. He was soon caught and bowled by Kippax bowled Fairfax for 10. It quickly became a procession with ten wickets falling in 35.4 overs. West Indies were all out for 107 and humiliated: overwhelmed by an innings and 122 runs. Between 1882 and 1912 there were ten instances of Tests finishing within two days. This one was one of the shortest, in terms of overs.

The Australian officials conferred with Grant and his colleagues and spelled out to them that the tour had been a financial disaster and economies had to be made. The first idea was to ask the tourists to pay for their travel, using public transport instead of taxis paid for by the Board. Grant had to agree. There was no alternative.

Just in time the luck turned in favour of the bedraggled West Indies. The last State game, the second played against NSW, swung their way with Fairfax, Oldfield and Archie Jackson all dropping out. Jackson was about to contract the disease, tuberculosis, which killed him two years later. It was one of the most tragi-romantic stories of Australian sport. He had moved to Brisbane, close to his lover Phyllis Thomas, a dancer, hopefully thinking that the warmer weather would help his condition. It didn't. He proposed to her while on his deathbed and died on the day when England regained the Ashes, aged twenty-three. Jack Fingleton, the Australian batsman who went on to become one of the outstanding cricket writers, always believed that Archie could have emulated the feats of Bradman had he survived.

Learie brought about an unexpected victory over the weakened NSW by scoring an uncharacteristic 41, followed up with 6–24, all bowled and flayed 93 in a hundred minutes in his second knock an innings which he rated his best on the tour. A rare century seemed his until wicketkeeper Davidson raced to square leg and hit the stumps leaving him well short of the batting crease. Victory by 86 runs was well received by the small crowd and the Australian Board officials were longing for a fair fight in the final Test, not another one-sided encounter.

Five of the Australians turned up late on the first day including Grimmett and Ironmonger. They spent thirty-six tiring hours on trains and arrived just in time to take the field. Ironmonger is still the second-oldest Test cricketer at the age of fifty years and 327 days. Wilfrid Rhodes was the eldest at fifty-two years and 165 days. The curator had produced a faster surface than usual and Grant, who won the toss and decided to bat, was delighted to see a pitch which suited his players. Freddie Martin (1895–1967), the solid Jamaican left-hander, batted through the day. Learie contributed nothing, a duck. Rain delayed the start next day with the West Indies on 298–2. As the sun came out the pitch became treacherous and Grant ordered a speed-up and with four wickets falling he gambled by declaring at 360–6 with Martin on 123*, helped by a classical 105 from George Headley. His boldness was rewarded: five Australians fell for 89. Only Bradman, 43, and Fairfax, 54, stuck at it. Several showers interrupted the action and Australia's laboured innings ended on 224.

The match was a timeless one but the tourists' boat was leaving on the Thursday; that left only one more day available.

Grant was determined to win and he took another daring gamble by declaring their second innings at 124–5, leaving Australia to score 251 on the final day. He was the first captain to declare twice in a Test. Learie dismissed openers Woodfull and Ponsford with catches and dismissed Kippax and Rigg.

Fairfax, 60*, fought on and with 31 runs needed, marched down the pitch to tell the last man, Ironmonger, to keep blocking the ball and let him to score the runs. 'We can still do it,' he said. Fairfax pushed the last ball of the over into the covers and called for a run. Not realising that Ironmonger was almost immobile, he careered on down the drying pitch, got in easily only to see that Bert was still only halfway down the runway, run out for four. It was an historic win by 30 runs and Learie summed it up in one of his books later: 'There are moments a man will never forget.' He never did.

The Australians loved him, so much so that someone signed a prominent artist to paint his portrait and it was hung in the pavilion at the Sydney ground. He came top of the tour bowling, taking 47 wickets for a cost of 20.23 apiece and came fourth in the batting with 708 runs for an average 30.78. In Tests, he could have done better but was proud to be labelled, by Bradman and others, 'the greatest all-round fielder in the world.'

The eminent cricket writer and broadcaster Alban George Moyes, better known as A.G. or Johnny (1893–1963), was more objective. He wrote in one of his nine books: 'Now and again he looked hostile. His fielding was a sight for the gods. Sometimes he hit well but our recollection is not one of achievement so much as of genius badly directed. Nevertheless, we can be glad of the genius. We recall his manner of playing cricket.'

The celebrations were muted after the match: they had to pack and make sure they were ready to catch the SS *Mataroa* next morning. On the way back to the Caribbean they had a champagne reception at Panama. Most of them returned to their islands. Jackie Grant went off to become a missionary. Learie went home to Nelson and he was a bit of a missionary himself in England's 'mountainous green and its pleasant pastures seen.'

EIGHT

CAUGHT UP WITH THE BODYLINE ROWS

During the MCC tour to the West Indies in 1925–6 Learie fell out with Wally Hammond and their feud lasted seven years. It started when the England team arrived and Learie thought Hammond was a bit of a snob and a racist. When they faced each other on the cricket field Learie and George John, who was almost as fast, bounced him and Hammond complained about their tactics. Lionel Tennyson told Hammond, 'Shut up and bat.' Wally didn't shut up.

When Learie hit the elderly George Gunn several times with more bouncers Hammond intervened and told him to play the game the right way. Learie was incensed. He always said that the short-pitched ball is a legitimate weapon on flat pitches. If the batsmen didn't fancy it they could take evasive action. Hammond (1903–1965) was one of England's greatest all-time cricketers but he wasn't a nice person. He was often moody, depressed, lacking of friends and treated women badly. His two marriages broke up and he had feuds with Charlie Barnett (1910–1993), the England and Gloucestershire cricketer who played for Rochdale in the Lancashire League and Don Bradman, among others.

No one doubted his cricketing abilities, his technically dynamic batting, medium-fast bowling and world-class fielding. He had a very unusual upbringing. Son of an Army corporal living in quarters of Dover Castle, who became a major and died in Amiens in the First World War, he went on to live with his family in Hong Kong and Malta. His mother, Marion (nee Crisp), wanted her son to go into farming but he preferred playing cricket. They moved to Portsmouth and Wally attended the local grammar school before his mother sent him as a boarder to Cirencester Grammar School. In a school game he scored 365.

That was where he caught the cricket bug. Instead of spending his holidays with his mother, he insisted on staying with friends. Gloucestershire signed him but having not been born in the county – he came from Kent – his registration was rejected and it took some time to restart his career. All these things may well have shaped his personality.

But a turning point in his life took place in British Guiana in 1926 when he went down with blood poisoning, allegedly from a bite from a mosquito. That distinguished *Guardian* journalist David Foot, who wrote an outstanding biography of Hammond, found evidence to suggest that he had syphilis, the disease which finished off the legendary founder of the *Daily Mail*, Lord Northcliffe. On the boat returning to England there was no doctor or medication and Hammond came close to death. He missed the coming season and for the rest of his life his career was dogged with illness. He went to South Africa to recuperate and he had an affinity with the white supremacy ideal.

His mother moved to Shanklin in the Isle of Wight and I interviewed her for the *Isle of Wight Guardian* in 1953. She was a nice person and she said she still loved him despite not seeing him. When he retired from playing cricket he settled in South Africa and found his businesses collapsing under him and became impoverished. In 1960 he had a serious car accident and five years later he died of a heart attack in Kloof in Natal at the age of sixty-two.

Hammond wasn't all bad. People like Pelham Warner and Lionel Tennyson encouraged him to adopt a sporting approach, playing in the right spirit, and in the 1932–3 Bodyline series in Australia he told Tim Wall, the Australian spearhead fast bowler, 'If that is what the bloody game's coming to, I've had enough of it.' The incidents in 1926 in the West Indies are generally thought to have given birth to the Bodyline concept – marking the batsmen as a target to be hit in their bodies.

England captain Douglas Jardine was the chief guilty party. He started the trouble Down Under by instructing his bowlers to bowl bouncers with a ring of close fielders on the legside, particularly at Bradman who didn't relish facing Harold Larwood's express speed bowling. With no means of recording the times of his deliveries, Larwood wasn't listed as one of the Fastest Fast Bowlers of all time. The fastest was Pakistan's Shoaib Akhtar at 100.2mph. Had Larwood (1904–1995) been accurately timed he would surely have been in the top ten, not far behind Akhtar.

Pictures of Bodyline matches show the short legs Jardine set were less intimidating than today's close fielders in terms of closeness. Usually the fielders were positioned up to ten yards from the batsmen, wearing their England caps or floppy white hats. They had no protection and if batsmen were about to play a hook shot they had more time to avoid being hit. Brian Close was the bravest of the brave when he stood two yards away from Gary Sobers at the Oval in 1966 when he caught him out off a rebound from his 'box'. These days short leg fielders wear shin pads, chest protectors and helmets. They crouch down low about four or five yards away and stay down and if a hook or a slog/sweep shot is played they expect to see the ball speeding away over their heads.

Larwood was only five feet eight inches tall and his bouncer came from a lower trajectory, making it even more dangerous than taller bowlers like Jeff Thomson, Brett Lee and Shaun Tait. I met Larwood at Trent Bridge on one of his visits from his home in Australia and he came over as a very gentle, kindly old man with a smile. You couldn't imagine him being responsible for the breakdown of relations between MCC and the Australian Board.

The controversy about Bodyline lingered on into 1933 when the West Indians toured England. Learie was thirty-two and wanted to take on England again but realised that Nelson, with his increased salary, would be reluctant to release him. Negotiations about his availability broke down when the other Lancashire League clubs objected on the grounds of losing money if he went off to play in Tests.

This tour to England would have been his last chance to pit himself against Larwood in the three Test series. Larwood returned from Australia with a fractured bone in his left foot and would have been fit but for MCC's cowardly decision to end his Test career, which embraced only twenty-one Tests. If anyone deserved to be sacked, it should have been Jardine. Half of Larwood's 1,427 first-class wickets were bowled – 743 – and he dismissed Bradman four times out of eight in that Bodyline series, a fact that Jardine claimed justified for his leg theory assault.

Was Jardine an ogre? The people who were close to him saw him differently from his critics. Everyone agreed that he was a complex character. A qualified solicitor, he went into banking and journalism when he prematurely retired at the age of thirty-four. At his funeral in 1958 after he died of pneumonia in Montreux, Switzerland, aged fifty-eight, another Winchester pupil, Sir Herbert Ashton, former MCC President, MP for Chelmsford, who married Dorothy, the sister of Hugh Gaitskell, said at the service: 'he was provocative, austere, shy, humble, kindly, sensitive, single-minded and possessed of immense moral and physical courage.' Raymond Robertson-Glasgow said of him: 'if he has been sometimes fierce, he has also been a wonderful friend.

Jardine sent out a nightwatchman, Walter Franklin, to open with Joseph Harold Anthony Hulme (1904–1991); Learie responded with a succession of bouncers, several of them bouncing off Hulme's torso. Joe complained bitterly before he managed to edge the ball to the keeper and walked off saying 'I know where I'm well off.' Joe was one of the best dual sportsmen in Britain, appearing in 225 matches for Middlesex and 333 matches for Arsenal as a right-winger. I knew him well because after he managed Tottenham Hotspur between 1945–9, he became a sports journalist. He didn't write much: he used a ghostwriter. But he was good at passing on tips about footballers being transferred. He was always cracking jokes.

Bill Bowes (1908–1987), the six-feet-four-inch-tall England and Yorkshire fast-medium swing bowler who played in the Melbourne Test in 1932 bowling Bradman out first ball, became a proper journalist when he retired. He was the cricket correspondent of the *Yorkshire Post*. He was very helpful in my career and he had the respect of both cricketers and journalists, as well as his readers. In WW2 he was captured at Tobruk in 1942 and spent three years in prisoner of war camps. During that time his weight of fifteen stone dropped to eleven.

Learie's partner in the MCC game was Emmanuel Alfred Martindale (1909–1972) from Barbados and his bowling was faster than Learie's. Skipper Jackie Grant ordered him to test out Patsy Hendren (1889–1962) on the next day, hitting him in various places, all painful. Manny Martindale was a typical nice Bajan and when Hendren went out to the middle wearing a home-made foam rubber cap – thought to be the first time a cricketer wore a helmet – he laughed. It probably spurred him on to bowl even faster. The *Daily Sketch* – my old newspaper – said his headwear was 'a cross between an airman's helmet and an Eskimo's headgear – ridiculous.' One of Learie's quicker deliveries nearly decapitated him. He just managed to sway out of line of the ball.

Hendren, a popular man who specialised in practical jokes and mimicry, explained that he was hit on the head four times in his career, once by a bouncer from Larwood that needed six stitches and explained, 'I still get headaches and I'm not going to take any more risks.' Learie took four wickets and scored a whirlwind half-century in twenty-seven minutes to help bring about a welcome win by 152 runs. A short time later, the MCC kept the Bodyline War bubbling along by cabling the Australian Board saying that the leg theory was not legitimate. There was talk of the Ashes series for the following year being cancelled to cool tempers. Peace had yet to be brokered.

Without the services of Learie, the First Test at Lords followed the pattern of the West Indies tour in Australia, another defeat by an innings, this time the margin was 27 runs. Leslie Ethelbert George Ames (1905–1990), the genial Kent wicketkeeper who collected a heap of records in his long career, came in at seven and top-scored with an unbeaten 83* in England's only innings of 296. The asterisk was a useful addition to his extremely worthy batting average of 40.56. West Indies managed a total of 97 with Robert Walter Vivian Robins (1906–1968) taking 6–32. 'Robby' was one of my best contacts and when he later became chairman of the selectors he often told me the names of the new players in advance. He was probably the most adventurous of England's captains and had a wonderful sense of humour. In the 1937 Test in Australia, Gubby Allen was bowling to Bradman early in his innings and asked him to move to fine leg before he bowled a short delivery. Bradman hooked, and Robby dropped the catch. Allen said, 'Don't give it a thought, you've probably cost us the Ashes.' Bradman went on to 270 and enabled Australia to win the Test and the series 3–2. In the second innings the West Indies mustered 172. Headley, on 50, was the only man to hold an end.

Learie was cleared to face Yorkshire at Harrogate and Grant reintroduced Bodyline to try to counter the doctoring of the pitch by the groundsman, as he thought, though the evidence didn't support his case. Learie captured nine wickets at the expense of 94 runs on a sluggish pitch which was ideally suited to the immaculate bowling of Hedley Verity (1905–1943). Grant deliberately set an intimidating close field for Learie and Griffith with five short legs but there was no pace in the pitch and the plan flopped. With Verity taking 14–83, Yorkshire won by 200 runs. It is doubtful whether there has been a better English slow left-arm bowler than Verity, of whom Christopher Martin-Jenkins said: 'He was a kindly, thoughtful and clean-living man.' A Captain in the Green Howards in the 8th army he died from wounds in Caserta, Italy in 1943 and his last words to his soldiers were 'Keep going.'

Learie was set to play against Lancashire but rain washed out the game and there was only one other fixture before the Second Test at Old Trafford for which he was available – taking on Sydney Barnes at Stoke on Trent. It was Sydney's last appearance against a touring side and he looked washed out. He was sixty and whereas Learie took 11–72, Barnes proved relatively expensive and hardly took a wicket. He was famous for his aloofness, his independence and his longevity. Both Barnes and Sir Stanley Matthews were men of Staffordshire and the smoke belching out from its factories didn't seem to harm them. When Sydney played his last League in his late sixties he carried on with his other trade, inscribing legal and official documents, into his nineties before he died aged ninety-four. His biographer claimed that he took 6,229 wickets at 8.33 apiece. Jimmy Anderson's 2661 is a long way behind at the time of writing!

Before the Test, Grant discussed the idea of using more short-pitched bowling and said Hammond, in particular, didn't fancy facing it. Without the services of Larwood and Voce, England were outgunned by Grant's pair of Learie and Martindale who were much faster than England's opening pair Edward Winchester 'Nobby' Clark (1902–1982), the Northamptonshire left-arm fast bowler who played eight Tests, and Yorkshire's George Gibson Macauley (1897–1940). The firm pitch suited pace and Grant didn't hesitate to bat first.

'Nobby' Clark aimed a lot of bumpers at George Headley who withstood them without fear because he was the best batsmen of his generation, brought up on hard West Indian pitches. Headley was 145* in a total of 333–6 at the close of play. The dogged Ivan Barrow (1911–1979), the twenty-two-year-old Jamaican opener, persevered to become the first Jamaican to score a Test hundred in England. He faced up England's best bowlers and survived but failed against the undemanding bowling of Bob Wyatt who bowled him for 105. Learie made a brisk 31 and Headley 169* was unbeaten and unbowed, in the second-highest innings the West Indies had achieved in their history – 375 scored at three an over.

The suave Herbert Sutcliffe was soon run out, basically by himself, for 20 and when Hammond came in, Martindale and Learie stepped up the number of bouncers. Trying to duck one from Learie, Hammond misjudged and was hit on the shoulder. Almost immediately another bouncer glanced off his chin, cutting it, and blood poured down his shirt. He had to go off for treatment. The team's trainer stuck a plaster on it and Hammond went back to the middle with loud applause. He walked purposely up to Learie, stretched his hand forward and said, 'Let's put an end to this, shall we?' Learie shook hands and smiled. The feud had ended. For the rest of Hammond's life – his ended seven years before Learie's – the two men had respect for each other. From that moment on, Learie refrained from bowling at Hammond's upper body and head.

Hammond didn't stay long: he was caught by Martindale off Learie's bowling for 34. Wyatt was magnificently caught by Learie off Martindale for 18 and at 134–4 England was tottering. Both bowlers had expended nearly all their energy, blunted by the courageous defensive technique of Jardine. They often used Jardine's Harlequin cap as a target and the gaunt, aquiline figure ducked or swayed out of range. If a throat ball was coming he would play it with a firm defensive shot. Jardine edged past the 100 mark, his first century in Tests, and Sutcliffe said, 'It was a classic innings and one of the best I have ever seen against a magnificent attack for an incredibly long time.' It was Test cricket at its very peak of achievement.

Les Ames stuck it out, helping out in a stand of 87. When the tension was at its height, Jardine walked up to him and said, 'You get down the other end, I'll take care of this bloody nonsense.' In one of his books, Learie wrote years later: 'The leg trap stuff didn't work, mainly because Jardine played it in the proper manner and stood up to it.' Jardine batted for five hours for his 127 and Learie and his colleagues clapped him in. If Grant had another genuinely fast bowler he might have forced a win but the third quick bowler, Vincent Adolphus Valentine (1908–1982), didn't frighten anyone.

George Macaulay fell and injured himself in the field and took no further part in the game. Martindale was flaking out himself and it was left to Ellis Edgar 'Puss' Achong (1904–1986), of mixed blood, English and Chinese, the Trinidadian left-arm slow bowler to finish off the innings at 374. Walter Robins could be classed as an all-rounder with one Test century and a batting average of 26.60 and 64 wickets, average 27.46 in his nineteen Tests. He had just reached his 50 when he charged down the pitch – he often did this! – and missed a delivery from Achong and was stumped several yards out of his ground. Piqued by throwing his wicket away when there was no batting left he spluttered, 'Fancy being done by a bloody Chinaman!' In today's PC world he would been charged for making a racist remark and sent off the field for ten overs. A word, namely 'Chinaman', went into cricketing lore to describe the left-armer's leg break where the ball turns from the off to right-handers. Denis Compton loved bowling them when he was given an opportunity.

Everyone laughed out in the middle and 'Puss' joined in. Despite his popularity with his colleagues, he was only allowed two Tests and his eight wickets were costly, 47.25 each. He settled down in Manchester and married and appeared for several Lancashire League clubs until he retired in 1951. In that time he took 1,000 wickets.

There was only one day's play remaining and few people turned up at the start, with little prospect of a result. It was the turn of England's slow left-arm bowler, James Langridge of Sussex (1906–1966), to show off his bowling, which included intermittent Chinamen while taking 7–56. At 132–7 the West Indies might have lost but a rumbustious 64 from Learie prevented that happening.

James Southerton, (1874–1935), the highly respected editor of *Wisden*, said of Bodyline: 'We can, at any rate, be thankful to the West Indies for showing us what an objectionable form of attack this kind of bowling can be. Most people in England, whichever way they are inclined, were to a large extent ignorant of the effect it had upon cricket, and there can be no doubt whatever that the exhibition at Old Trafford confirmed it in their views and caused hundreds who had open minds on the subject, definitely to turn against it.'

Two years later Southerton had just toasted 'Cricket' at the annual dinner of the Ferrets CC at the Oval when he fell to the ground and died within minutes. A cricketer of lesser ability, he was the son of Sydney, the famed England round arm bowler from Mitcham, who made his debut for the side at forty-nine and 119 days. He was still playing in his fifties before he, too, suddenly died of pleurisy.

Grant was determined to include Learie in his side for the Third and last Test at the Oval and Nelson lined up Morris Stanley Nicholls,(1900–1961), the all-rounder of Essex who started his sporting life as a goalkeeper with QPR, to play in the Saturday League match at Seedhill. Jardine was believed to be the person who stopped the plan, by asking the selectors to choose Nicholls for the Test in place of the stricken Macaulay. So Learie had to play for Nelson. These three Tests were scheduled for three days and on another featherbed pitch the West Indies were undone on the Monday after England piled on 312. It rained and soaked the pitch. As the sun came out, they were hustled out for 100 in just under two hours. Following on, they had eight batsmen in double figures and only one, Roach, with 56, tried to hold up an end. They were painlessly dismissed for 195, losing by an innings and 17 runs.

The star, Headley, failed twice but he had an excuse. He missed several games after having a suspicious cyst removed from his forehead – which thankfully wasn't malignant – and the aunt who brought him up being killed in a hurricane. Learie's verdict was: 'Once more, the same old story, some of our best men were left behind, not nearly enough play together before the tour to weld us into a team – we were more like a mob.'

Charles Stowell, (1895–1966), the Lancashire-born Cambridge Blue leg-spin bowler from Kent, did the damage with a match analysis of 11–96, still the best tally for a one Test appearance, at the age of thirty-seven. Both Marriott and

Langridge were quality bowlers and in today's cricket they would have had many more Tests. In the 1930s spin bowlers of all types - except doosra exponents - abounded in county cricket, playing on rain-affected pitches. Once the covers went on and county committees insisted on hard, flat surfaces treated with glue, spinners became a rare breed.

After Learie's jaunt to India with the Maharajah's cricketing friends at the end of the year, he received a telegram from the West Indian selectors asking him to play in the home series against MCC in 1934–5. He readily accepted the rather mean financial terms and decided to travel by boat to Port of Spain with Norma and Gloria. Norma hadn't been back to Trinidad for some years and welcomed the idea. The England players had just celebrated Christmas on another boat close to Barbados and the First Test was about to start on January 8th. The lengthy journey meant Learie wouldn't be available until the Second Test in Port of Spain beginning on the 24th.

Had he been in Barbados earlier - the Board should have arranged a flight for him - the West Indies may have been victors in a low-scoring game interrupted by a succession of short, sharp showers which kept the pitch in a bowler-friendly state for the three days. The match was the first to have three declarations in a Test. Only Headley, whose 44 was the highest individual score in the match, managed to eke out his innings as England bowled his side out for 102. Ken Farnes (1911–1941) was looked on as a natural successor to Harold Larwood and though he wasn't as quick through the air, his six-feet-five-inch height made him almost unplayable, taking 4–40. Farnes, who was called up by the RAF as a pilot, only played fifteen Tests and died in 1941 after his aircraft crashed at Chipping Warden in Oxfordshire.

Jardine had retired and Bob Wyatt was the new skipper. Only Hammond, with 43, was able to counter the new West

Indian opening attack of Martindale and the debutant Leslie Hylton (1905–1955). Both took three wickets. Realising that the pitch might dry out quickly, Wyatt declared at 81–7. Grant followed his example, changed his batting order and declared on 75–6 leaving England to score just 73 runs. Martindale whipped out Maurice Leyland, Patsy Hendren, Errol Holmes, C.I.J. Smith and G.A.E. Paine and England were in peril at 43–5. Wyatt also astutely changed his batting order, sending in Farnes as an opener – Farnes only made five – and Hammond, at six, and himself at eight, and together they saw England through to victory by four wickets as the pitch eased.

On May 17th in 1955 Hylton was the first cricketer to be hanged for murder at the Spanish Town Prison in St. Catherine in Jamaica. He fell in love with Lurline Rose, daughter of a police inspector, and despite opposition from her father, the pair were married in 1942. She subsequently went to live in New York and when he visited her he found a letter from a Roy Francis, who was in a relationship with Lurline. Hylton was enraged. They eventually patched up their marriage and Lurline returned to Jamaica to live with Hylton. Subsequently he found another incriminating letter from Francis. Consumed with jealousy, he produced a gun and shot Lurline six times, killing her. At the court case Hylton claimed he was trying to shoot himself, not her, and the jury didn't believe his story. He was aged fifty. A thick, heavy-set man who bowled at a considerable speed, Hylton played in all four Tests taking thirteen wickets at 19.3 apiece: a laudable achievement.

The next West Indian series took place in England in 1939 and after dismissing Len Hutton for 196 at Lord's he was dropped after the second Test and at thirty-four was discarded. His tally of six Tests was matched by the number of bullets he fired to kill his wife.

Learie was greeted with great enthusiasm when he appeared in two warm-up matches on the newly installed jute matting at the Queen's Park Oval. He hadn't played in Trinidad since 1930 because, as a professional, he wasn't picked in intercolonial matches. Both matches were exciting encounters and the highlight in the second one, playing for the first time for the colony with his brother Elias, put on 93 in a torrent of sixes, almost snatching an unlikely victory.

The substandard England attack struck early in the Test when Wyatt decided to field but James Edward Derek Sealy (1912–1982) who at the age of seventeen and 122 days was the youngest West Indian Test player in 1930, revived the innings with an elegant 92. He failed to realise all of his promise and finished up teaching at the famous Combermere School in Barbados and Frank Worrell was one of his pupils. Learie punished Wyatt's exhausted bowlers and next day, he was well on his way to his first Test century. Caution was needed but he continued hitting out and was caught by Hendren off a skier. His 90 proved to be his highest Test score. The West Indies total of 302 appeared unreachable when England found themselves at 23–5 with Hylton having Wyatt and Hammond caught by Grant's brother Rolph Stewart Grant (1909–1977). Rolph won Blues at Cambridge, for cricket and football. He later became goalkeeper for the England amateur side and was also Trinidad's heavyweight boxing champion. Not a man to be insulted on the field.

Errol Reginald Thorold Holmes (1909–1960), a tall, right-handed batsman born in Calcutta who learnt his cricket at Malvern and Oxford University and copied Jardine's preference in wearing the Harlequin cap, was number eight and saved the day with his unbeaten 85, hoisting the all-out score to 258. Holmes was an outstanding representative of well-off Oxbridge players in that era, who played for enjoyment and were not worried about money. Out of season he worked in the Stock Exchanges of London and New York and when Jardine retired as captain of Surrey in 1934, he was walking along Throgmorton Street when he bumped into Henry Dudley Gresham Leveson-Gower (1893–1954), the Surrey President known as Shrimp. Shrimp was one of twelve sons of Granville Gresham Leveson-Gower and he went to Oxford as well and was a stockbroker. He offered him the captaincy of Surrey and Holmes readily agreed. One of his first decisions was to ban Bodyline at the Oval. In WW2 he made countless bombing raids over Germany in the US Bomb Wing Division as a flak expert in Boeing B-17 Flying Fortresses and was awarded the US version of the DFC. The durable B-17s were renowned for their ability to return to their bases in East Anglia full of holes caused by flak. Jack Hobbs said of him, 'He is a lovely fellow and wouldn't tolerate shady or underhand behaviour.'

England's indifferent bowling helped Headley to bolster his side's second innings with his 93 and Learie was frustrated by Wyatt's tactics of bowling wide outside the off stump. He had to work hard to add 31. The crowd rose to 11,000, a record in a West Indies Test in the Caribbean, and Grant declared at 280–6 leaving England to score 325 in 210 minutes. A writer in the *Trinidad Guardian* said, 'there might still be a chance of an exciting finish.' Wyatt almost reversed his batting order, sending in his usual numbers ten and eleven, Farrimond and Paine, to handle the onslaught of Martindale and Hylton. Both men soon perished and only another ex-Winchester College and Oxford University man David Charles Humphrey Townsend (1912–1997), from Norton-on-Tees, showed character to hold firm for his 36 before he fell to the wiles of Achong. A defensive-minded batsman, he succeeded in hitting the only six of the innings. He was the last man to have represented his country without having played for a first-class county.

Learie claimed the prize wicket of Hammond, nine, coming in at five instead of his usual three and with Ames, six, Hendren run out for 11, and Jack Iddon, 0, all failing, it was left to Maurice Leyland, relegated from five to nine, to mount one of his famous rearguard actions. Learie soon had him dropped and responded by bowling bouncers. Under the consensual agreement about Bodyline, Grant took him off. The crowd booed. They wanted him to continue. With time running out, Grant brought him back. Once more he saw Leyland dropped. As someone who never swore he must have been tempted. Holmes came in at eleven. Learie bowled off a short run to squeeze in another over or more. Holmes played out Hylton's last over and it was now up to Learie to get rid of Leyland to win the first Test victory of the West Indies. The first four deliveries went by or were blocked. Learie turned to his mark and charged up to the wicket and reversed his right hand enabling him to reduce the speed of the ball. This skill is now commonplace, especially in T20, but Learie was one of the pioneers of it. Leyland played too soon and the slower delivery slanted into Leyland's front pad. Learie and his fielders leapt up appealing, and with the crowd on their feet and cheering him on, the pressure was on Arthur Richardson (1888–1979), the Australian Test player now umpire who stood in three of the Tests as a neutral umpire. Slowly he put up his finger – out! 'Ten thousand people rushed on to the pitch,' said Learie. 'We tried to dodge but it was no good. I found myself shoulder high, swaying and bumping amidst yells and laughter. It was one of the moments when one sipped nectar with the Gods.' His figures were 14.5–9–11–3. It was the only second Test match held at Port of Spain and the next one took place fourteen years later.

The third Test at Bourda, Georgetown, was an anticlimax played on a moribund pitch. The lively Hylton out-bowled Martindale and Learie as England scraped to 226 in 133 overs at 1.99 an over. The West Indies matched their abysmal scoring rate in making 184 at 1.98 per over. It must have been dire watching it. Wyatt declared on 160–6 in the second innings – this time scored at two an over – and Learie lost patience and went down the pitch and was stumped by Ames for seven. The match petered out (104–5) to a draw.

A restful sea journey to Kingston from Georgetown, 1,474 miles from the two furthest parts of the Caribbean cricketing countries, revived enthusiasm among Grant's players, especially George Headley. Dropped off an easy chance to square leg by Ken Farnes on 70, he went on to an unbeaten 270 in the West Indies 535–7. It was a pity that Learie was lbw for 34 because he hit the only two sixes in the innings. Ames, with 126, scored almost half of England's 271 when Learie made another headline-making catch to dismiss him. He captured six wickets in the match to hasten a humiliating defeat for England of an innings and 161 runs. Wyatt was forced to retire when a fast, rising ball from Martindale struck him in the jaw, cracking a bone. Errol Holmes, the vice captain, reassured everyone it was a 'perfectably fair ball'. Grant twisted his ankle in the field and asked Learie to take over the captaincy. Learie celebrated by taking another cracking catch just five feet away from Patsy Hendren.

The *Jamaican Daily Gleaner* cricket writer wrote an almost Shakespearean tome about him: 'Sealy was followed by Constantine, the greatest and most attractive personality in cricket the West Indies ever had. His spectacular batting arouses joy and excitement in all crowds. His bowling is always productive of some rare feat that makes people sit up and laugh themselves crying. His fielding with its unbounded energy, long striding catlike leaps and marvellous accuracy in effecting the most inconceivable catches and gathering of balls, just fascinates. Some of his work is essentially of Constantine's exclusive manufacture, there being no necessity for taking copyright or forbidding limitations. Will we ever again have a player like this?'

It was the first series win and he was eulogised at a reception at the Governor's House. His summary about his final cricket match in Jamaica ran: 'and then to bed, to live it all over and over again in dreams, never to escape from the shattering roar of the crowd, continuous and splendid.' The next day he took a taxi to Port Antonio to board the banana boat SS *Camito* to Bristol to resume playing for Nelson.

Peter Mason said in his book about him: 'Given the measures the West Indian authorities had taken to ensure that no black man would ever captain a regional side it was a great irony and a huge source of delight to Constantine that he should be the man to lead the team at the moment of their greatest achievement so far.' Learie's contribution in the series was 169 runs with an average of 33.80 and 15 wickets at 13.13.

NINE

LEARIE'S SWANSONG IN TESTS

The world-renowned Australian Nellie Melba's swansong lasted eight years up until 1928 but Learie's lasted just three months. His contribution in the three Test series in 1939 was modest: 110 runs, 12 wickets and one catch but the West Indies, though losing the series 1–0, put up tremendous resistance. That quality was needed shortly afterwards when the civilised world finally woke up to realise the full meaning of the warmongering rants of Adolf Hitler and 'The Horst Wessel Song', the Nazi anthem.

On September 3rd, two weeks after the final Test at the Oval ended in a high-scoring draw, Prime Minister Neville Chamberlain announced that Britain was now at war after Germany failed to respond to his ultimatum to withdraw German troops from Poland. Learie didn't serve in the armed forces but remained in Nelson, and then to Liverpool to work as a civil servant to help the war effort. As an inspiring, great sportsman he was more valuable in the Liverpool docks than on the front line. Thousands of West Indians volunteered to come over to either serve in the armed forces or unload the war material and fill the gaps in factories where so many Englishmen were called up. Having someone of his sporting aura to guide them was a huge psychological boost.

There were no more West Indian Test series after the momentous first victory over England in 1935 until the visit to England in 1939. In the previous year Learie had moved to Rochdale, who paid him £800 for a twenty-week season. A number of other West Indian Test players were jealous of his earnings and many years later this was still mentioned around the Caribbean cricketing clubs. The older players pointed out his averages in his eighteen Tests – 641 runs at just 19.42 with no centuries and 58 wickets at 30.10. But they overlooked his dynamism on the field and his appeal to the public.

In 1938 his friend Harry Mallett volunteered to help his negotiations with the West Indian Board about Learie's salary while he was about to end his contract with Rochdale and undertake what he thought would be his last Test series at the age of thirty-eight. Learie knew the value of money and wanted proper remuneration. The Board's first offer was around £500 for each of the three professionals. The others were on expenses of £250 plus £50 for kit. Learie said he wanted more. He knew he was the main attraction and he had to return to Barbados from England to continue the argument. The sum of £800 was too high and he settled on £600 with a percentage from the profits of £4,684 from the 1939 tour.

The sum of £800 in 1938 was the equivalent to £50,960 according to the government's Retail Price Index in 2017, roughly the same as the average weekly wage of Premiership footballers, but there are other factors to take into account. The sum of the value of labour in the UK was now worth £139,000 and the value of income rose to £240,000. Unlike today's footballers, there was no TV money available to enhance the salaries of pre-WW2 cricketers, and no money from advertising. The only other possible avenue was to pick up moderate sums from newspapers. W.G. Grace and Jack Hobbs did but it is unlikely that Learie was asked. Instead, he embarked on writing cricketing books designed to appeal to young, aspiring cricketers. None topped the bestsellers but they were well written and well reasoned, particularly *Colour Bar*.

Early in February the selection panel of Lt-Col William Bowring MBE (of the 1900 West Indies team) chaired the meeting and its members were Vernon Dias of British Guiana, Jack Kelshall of Trinidad, Noel 'Crab' Nethersole of Jamaica and skipper Rolph Grant. None were black. There were nine new caps. The average age of the side in the First Test was twenty-six years and four months.

The higgledy-piggledy way of bringing the squad together was typical of West Indies cricket at the time. On April 11th the Trinidad players sailed to Bridgetown on the MV *Columbia*. The next day, joined by Clarke, Sealey, Williams and the manager Jack Kidney, they sailed across the Atlantic and arrived in Plymouth on April 21st. Learie and Martindale were already in England. The first match was supposed to be played at the private ground of the historic village of Busbridge, near Godalming in Surrey, which currently has a population of around 800, but it was rained off.

Learie had been in a strong position to negotiate for his final contract for a West Indian tour and the Board agreed he was to be the senior professional. His chances of becoming the first black captain were nil. Grant, despite his alleged lack of professionalism, remained in charge. Learie hankered for the vice-captain position but again, he was overlooked. The appointee was the light-skinned John Hemsley Cameron (1914–2000), son of a doctor, John Joseph Cameron, who lived in the West Country. His father played for Jamaica and Somerset and took part in an unofficial West Indies series in 1906. John Junior was born in Kingston and was educated at Taunton School and went on to Cambridge University and gained three successive Blues. He bowled big turning leg breaks and when they were punished, he switched to prodigious off breaks.

He starred when he was picked for an England XI when he took 10–49 against a Public Schools XI. He played a few games for Jamaica and a number with Somerset as an amateur and his record couldn't compare to the first-class figures of Elias, Learie's brother, who scored 895 runs with an average of 27.12 and took 24 wickets at 36.33 for Trinidad. Elias was never capped but was good enough to play with Learie for Rochdale and stayed on in England and remained there. When there was a chance of him making the 1939 tour he paid his own expenses to Trinidad hoping to play in the warm-up games, but wasn't chosen. Learie had urged the selectors to take him even though he was thirty-seven and past his best. He died at Brondesbury on his ninety-first birthday in 2003.

Evidently, the colour of skin still counted. Cameron Junior scored 1, 0 and 5 in his two Tests (coming in as six, ahead of Learie at eight at the Old Trafford Test) and his three wickets – a renowned trio of Harold Gimblett, Eddie Paynter and Wally Hammond – cost 30 apiece. He was then dropped, forever. I met him in the early 1960s and he was a true gentleman.

The other leg-spinner who made the tour was a black doctor named Carlos Bertram Clarke (1918–2003). A man with great charm, I met him on a number of occasions with Learie and he was universally popular. Born at Bridgetown, he stayed on in London after the tour to qualify as a doctor at Guy's Hospital. Some years later he was in trouble with the police after performing some 'mercy' abortions. The law had yet to be passed to permit abortions on certain conditions but his 'crime' was soon excused and he once was presented to Queen

Elizabeth. He was twenty-one when he was selected for the tour and George Headley recommended him after his performances in the trial matches in preference to Ellis Achong. He appeared in the Old Trafford and Oval Tests and his figures were slightly better than Cameron's – three runs, average one, and six wickets at 43.50. The West Indians failed to produce a top-class spinner until Sonny Ramadhin and Alf Valentine came in the 1950s and Lance Gibbs in the 1960s with Gibbs as their best ever performer. One of his many records was to bowl the fastest overs ever, well under two minutes to bowl maidens. He sent down 27,115 deliveries, conceded 8,989 runs and took 309 wickets at 29.09.

During WW2 cricket was only played for three days a week and Clarke, known as Bertie, played in many of them, taking a total of 665 wickets for various sides, including the British Empire XI, BBC, various jazz-hat teams and in charity games often with Learie, who became a firm friend. His doctor's practice in the East End must have been a large one to enable him to play so much cricket. He was a familiar voice on the BBC's World Service programmes and was still playing the game into his seventies, still prising out batsman with his tempting loop and spin.

MCC's committee was apprehensive of granting five five-day Tests for Grant's team in view of the side's hardly impressive form in the international arena. So they chopped it down to three Tests of three days: rather mean! Had the International Cricket Council been in force, they would have intervened, but MCC were autocratic in those days. The Imperial Cricket Conference, set up in 1909, had just three members, England, Australia and South Africa, all white men ruling from Lord's overseeing mainly white players. It took eighty years to try to reform cricket's world organisation before the International Cricket Council took over. Today it has 104 countries with players of all colours and shades. Democracy has still yet to emerge because corruption, mainly from the Far East members, lingers on despite having committees including former corruptible ex-cricketers. Sadly, money talks.

Leslie Hylton was left out but Ernest Rae, the deputy chairman called on his Jamaica Cricket Board to make representations to the West Indies Board to reinstate the fiery Hylton. He also wanted another Jamaican, Donald Lacy, as assistant manager. the West Indies Board pleaded impoverishment and agreed, reluctantly, to take Hylton but not Lacy. Mallett might have won the argument but he fell ill; he didn't go on the trip and died in November. The reinstatement of Hylton turned out to be a sound decision because the speed of the bowling of Learie and Manny Martindale had slowed down.

On the boat from Trinidad Learie was buoyed up with the thought of starting his one and only first-class season of cricket as opposed to one-day cricket. But his joy on arrival was tempered by the coldest and wettest spring for forty-five years with harbours iced over at Bognor Regis, Folkestone and Southampton. The Serpentine became a huge ice rink. He said, 'It was a blue-faced and shivering mob which stepped thankfully off the boat and once they were here the weather moved steadily back towards mid winter.' One practice session was stopped by a snowstorm.

Following tradition, the opening first-class match took place at Worcester. The ground was underwater early in the year and by late April the square was just playable. Wearing two or three sweaters, Grant's bowlers dismissed the home side for 83 only to be beaten by 85 runs in two days. The only batsman to offer a challenge was Learie with 47. It was slightly warmer at Liverpool where Headley topped the scores and Cameron impressed with his leggies. In a short innings, played in difficult conditions, Learie hit the ball past square leg through his legs. He was criticised for showing off but he excused himself saying it struck a psychological blow to the bowlers. A generation later, that shot was almost commonplace, particularly in the IPL in India.

Grant, fielding close, was hit painfully in the shin and went off. Learie took over the leadership and with his side needing 247 to win in 185 minutes he urged caution. He told his players, 'We can't afford another beating so be careful.' It was against his normal gung-ho attitude but if the tour flopped the players wouldn't qualify for a bonus. The light was murky and though the West Indies still had seven wickets in hand, the match petered out in a draw.

Learie was reprimanded by manager Jack Kidney for being too negative and with Grant unfit for the MCC match that followed, Cameron was appointed skipper. The match was virtually washed out. Headley scored an authoritative hundred at Cambridge University while Learie hit form with 7–94 in a drawn match. Defeat followed at the Oval by seven wickets against Surrey, with Learie tonking a half-century in an hour. The form of West Indies fluctuated, mainly downwards, beating Oxford and then going down at Glamorgan where Learie scored 63 batting at nine and capturing 6–123. One of his sixes kayoed a spectator who needed first aid. Grant called a crisis meeting and warned his men that any more defeats would lead to a poor attendance at the First Test at Lords. Learie responded energetically, removing 13 Essex batsmen at a cost of 91 at Chelmsford and Essex were beaten by two wickets.

At Lord's against Middlesex, West Indies piled up 665 with Headley top-scoring with 227, with Derek Sealey making 181 and Jeff Stollmeyer 117. The sun was shining and it lifted their spirits, so much so that they won by an innings and 228 runs against one of England's outstanding counties. By this time Learie was experimenting with different types of slower bowling to avoid muscle strains if he put too much effort in his bowling. Bertie Clarke said, 'He wasn't the fast bowler of earlier years. He became a graceful medium-pace bowler who got his wickets by subtle change of pace and by a beautifully concealed slower googly. He retained the ball in his left hand unduly long, transferring it to his raised right arm at the last moment, and looking up as he did so. The flinging of arms and the unorthodox direction of his head was calculated to deceive a batsmen and it did so.'

Grant's side played in eleven matches, nine against counties and the two Oxbridge XIs, before the First Test at Lord's, somewhat different today when a tourist side can expect only one or two weakened opponents. The bookmakers made England firm favourite for the series, taking into account recent monumental batting achievements. After Len Hutton led the way with his world record of 364 in their 903–7 it was followed with totals of 422, 291–4, 559–9, 469–4, 215, 203–4, 326 and 654–5 in South Africa. It represented an average total of 640 in a completed innings. Hutton, Harold Gimblett, who later committed suicide, Denis Compton, Eddie Paynter, Wally Hammond, Bill Edrich and Joe Hardstaff – has there been a stronger England batting line-up?

The BBC gave ball-by-ball commentary of the play and another first at Lord's was an England captain, Hammond, speaking over the loudspeakers asking young men to volunteer to serve in the armed forces in readiness for the inevitable outbreak of war against Germany. As an omen of doom, thunderclaps were heard around NW8. Grant opted to bat against England's unbalanced attack. The two Bills, Bowes and Copson (1908–1971) did all the quick bowling with Hedley Verity, Doug Wright and Denis Compton bowling spin. The red-haired Copson was a former coal miner who was one of a distinguished line of English fast medium bowlers before and after WW2. His first ball in county cricket bowled Andy

Sandham and his Test career was limited to just three Tests in the 1939 series.

Copson's debut was outstanding – 5–85 in the first innings of the West Indies and 4–67 in the second. Only George Headley held him at bay. Headley, with 106, and the stylish Jeff Stollmeyer (1921–1989) making a debut at the age of eighteen with 59, took the total in poor light to 147–2 before the last six wickets fell for 51 runs: West Indies were all out 277 on a good batting surface. Stollmeyer was a white man, the youngest of six brothers from a prominent family in Port of Spain, who went on to become a Senator and leading cricket administrator before he was shot in a robbery at his house in 1989. Two men shot him five times and he was flown to Melbourne in Florida for treatment for gunshot wounds but died aged sixty-nine.

Day Two of the Test saw the sun burst out and Hutton, painstakingly crawling to 196, and Denis Compton, with a cavalier 120, put on 248 for England's fourth wicket after Hutton, once, and Compton, twice while on one, were dropped. Learie failed to take a wicket, Martindale was almost a spent force, Hylton was soon to be dropped and the leg-spinners Cameron and Clarke lacked penetration. Compton, England's new superstar, made his debut at the age of nineteen and 83 days, the third youngest English Test player against New Zealand two years earlier. Absent-minded, flamboyant and prolific, he caught the imagination of the public for twenty years, mostly in hard times for the nation. He provided a tonic to cheer people up. Hutton, shrewd, cautious and dogged, was the opposite but he did have a sense of humour, which I experienced many times when I encountered him.

Hammond declared on 404–5 at almost four an over. No one was able to partner Headley in the West Indies second innings and Sealey, 29, was the next highest scorer as wickets kept falling. Headley went into his defensive mode and that helped

England's momentum. When he finally reached his second century he became the first player to score a second hundred in each innings of a Test at Lord's. Trying to retain the strike he checked his shot against Wright and lobbed up a simple catch to Hutton. His 107 should have been much more. England was left 110 minutes to score 100 runs to win and they achieved it at a cost of two wickets with thirty-five minutes to spare.

Learie bowled three mean overs but it was too late. Stollmeyer, who wrote an erudite autobiography and penned a number of articles during his career, described his second innings dismissal for 17 like this: 'Learie guided an arm ball from Verity into the safe hands of Wally Hammond at slip, a diabolical stroke undoubtedly conceived in advance and played at the wrong moment. When he came into the dressing room his younger colleagues gathered round and asked the inevitable question: "Learie, what happened?" "Well, it was the in-swinger," he replied vaguely. Every time thereafter one of us got out playing a bad shot and was questioned, our standard answer was, "Well, it was the in-swinger."' Over the years, Learie didn't have a happy relationship with Stollmeyer.

Confidence zoomed as Nottinghamshire was pummelled by Headley, 234, and Sealy, 115, and Learie taking 9–117 in a one-sided contest. Rain, and even sleet, intervened in high summer and five successive matches ended in draws. At Harrogate, Headley took on Hedley Verity on a 'sticky dog' pitch which was ideal to suit Verity's unique form of bowling, quicker than the usual slow left-armers. Neville Cardus called Headley's 61 'the finest I've ever seen.' In the second innings Headley was unbeaten for 44 in his team's 116–6 to achieve a draw. The contest won between the two men was won by Headley as Verity only took five wickets of the 16 that were taken. Learie also starred, taking three wickets in an over while taking 5–28. This type of cricket – batsmen holding on against spitting, bouncing, turning deliveries – is never seen today because of covered pitches. In its way, it was more entertaining than seeing batsmen with blunderbuss bats smashing the ball constantly to the boundary.

The selectors took Verity's alleged failure to end his Test career at the age of thirty-four, replacing him with Gloucestershire's Thomas William John Goddard (1900–1966) who was five years older at the Old Trafford Test. Tom should have been called up many years earlier when he was on his way to becoming the fifth highest wicket taker of English bowlers, 2,979. He was still playing in county cricket at fifty when he caught pneumonia and was forced to retire. In the following year he made a brief comeback in a bid to reach his target of 3,000 and even took 10 wickets in an innings. He didn't quite make it before he died at sixty-six.

With Arctic weather reappearing, Grant told Hammond he wanted to bowl and there was only thirty-five minutes of play. Hammond took to the microphone calling for volunteers to join up and Learie made everyone laugh saying, 'He was addressing the right stuff, for only the lion-hearted remained to watch in the appalling conditions.' At lunch, England added just 23 runs to the 11 scored the day before. Soon England was 62–5. Compton slipped on the wet pitch and hit his wicket, on four, and Hutton, astonishingly dropped by Learie off a dolly, caught for 13. Grant preferred to stick to his spinners and Learie was only allowed seven overs to collect just one wicket. Joe Hardstaff's stoical 76 moved the total up to 164–7 before Hammond declared to give the tourists an hour and a quarter at the crease. Three wickets went down, for 85.

One day was left and Bill Bowes took advantage of it, rushing to snatch 6–33, hustling Grant's side out for 133. Goddard dismissed both openers and his four overs cost an astronomical 10 an over. Learie was bowled by Bowes round his legs for a duck and much later, Stollmeyer wrote, 'He was, when batting, inclined to meditate and decide what he would do before the bowler bowled, not always with the desired results.' In his *Guardian* report, Cardus joked, 'Only a clever pedestrian could have got his legs out of the way.'

Hammond wanted quick runs and Learie – his figures were 11–1–42–4 – restricted them to 128 when the skipper declared leaving the West Indies to score 160 in seventy minutes – almost eight an over. Fifteen overs were bowled and umpire Frank Chester called it off at 4:34 pm. Most of the three days were spent in the dressing rooms… and the spectators didn't get refunds. Learie summed it up as 'a game to be forgotten.'

Six more county sides were packed into the programme before the Final Test took place on August 19th, 21st and 22nd at the Oval. The first opponents were Surrey and it proved to be a confidence-booster for Grant's batsmen who rattled up 487 with Kenneth Hunnell Weekes (1912–1998) bludgeoning 146 and Headley eased his way to 93. Weekes, no relation of Everton, was an unusual character. His mother was Bajan and his father was a Jamaican and he was born in Boston and became the first eligible Test player from the USA although he never played for the US team. Known as 'Bam Bam' he was a left-hander who was renowned for his unorthodox slogging, 'like a mule' said Cardus. He only played two Tests in 1939 and after WW2 he retired from cricket and became a hospital nurse. On a typical dry Oval pitch Bertie Clarke took nine wickets at a cost of 144 runs and West Indies won by seven wickets.

Most of the journeys were in charabancs, as they were called before they were coaches, and a pleasant journey through the New Forest took the overjoyed players to Dean Park, Bournemouth. Bertie found Hampshire's pitch similar to the Oval and he had another big haul – thirteen wickets for 107 runs – enabling his team to win by ten wickets. Somerset's opening bowlers were far better than Hampshire's and William

'Bill' Harry Russell Andrews (1929–1999) with 6–40 and Arthur Wellard (1902–1980) with 4–43 shot out the tourists for 84 and after making 189 in their second innings, they went down to an innings and 72-run margin.

Wellard and Andrews were great characters. I knew Arthur and he was a champion of six hitting. 'More than 500,' he would say. It is doubtful whether Learie outdid him though. Bill made himself famous by calling his autobiography *The Hand that Bowled Bradman* published in 1972. Bradman was on 202 when he drove the ball back to him and held on to the catch. He often claimed that Bradman gave his wicket away. One doubts that!

Learie was in the wickets on a less dry, low bounce pitch at Swansea for the second match against Glamorgan. (Yes, the tourists played against several counties twice). The atmosphere helped his swing and the county only made 127 and 156 with Learie capturing 4–33 and 5–32 in a two-wicket win. The next appearance on cricket's treadmill was at Edgbaston and tired minds and bodies contributed to a low-scoring draw against Warwickshire.

The final county match before the Third Test at the Oval was at their Cheltenham College ground and Learie loved playing there. The tents and marquees were a welcome change to the often drab county grounds. Once again he found the target, bowling out five batsmen for only 40 runs. One victim was one of my favourite cricketers, Edward Desmond Richard Eagar (1918–1977), born nearby in Cheltenham, who played for Gloucestershire before WW2 and afterwards captained Hampshire. He wasn't an outstanding batsman but a fantastic leader of men. Almost everything he did on the cricket field was accompanied with a laugh and a quip. You could imagine him making a jocular remark when Learie removed his leg stump when he was on 15. Known as Desmond, he was the father of the much-admired cricket photographer Patrick Eagar. In another low-scoring game, Gloucestershire won by seven wickets to lower the confidence of Grant's overworked side.

The final match of the season for the tourists was the Third Test at the Oval. Six other fixtures in their scheduled thirty-six matches were cancelled after the declaration of war. Learie wrote about the scene: 'Over the Oval ground hung silvery shapes of cruel omen, barrage balloons flying above in case the German bombers should drone overhead during the match and make an unheralded attack on London at play. There was the drone of flying to be heard, unusual in London then; khaki and naval blue and a sprinkling of RAF uniforms showed everywhere among the crowds and as we approached the ground I saw gunners ostentatiously moving ack-ack guns by means of a tractor. Later we were told this story was to deceive German spies into mistaking London's four guns for a large number. There was feverish hurry at the stations and despite the sunshine, one saw sad and frightened faces. August 1939, Test match cricket – and death hovering in the air with a shadow everywhere.'

There was no sign of death out in the middle. Hammond won the toss and promptly decided to bat on one of the Oval's trademark pitches – flat and with the ball going through without much exaggerated movement. The tall left-arm fast bowler Tyrell Fabian Johnson (1917–1985) from Trinidad opened in preference to Learie and having taken his first-class wicket off his first ball at Worcester, he followed up by performing the same feat – Nottinghamshire's Walter Keeton bowled by his first delivery. That was his first and only Test match, yet another cricketer having his career sliced off by WW2. He was no relation to Hophnie Hobah Hines Johnson (1910–1987) of Jamaica who was faster and taller, who played in the 1950 tour of England.

England's debutant from Lancashire Norman 'Buddy' Oldfield, a short, right-handed opener with style, contributed

80 for the second wicket for 131 with Len Hutton, who was caught and bowled by Johnson for 73. Oldfield, too, was victim of Hitler's war because that was his only Test match. Coming on at first change, Learie switched to bowling sharpish off-spin and took out the middle order – Oldfield, Hammond for 43, Hardstaff 94, Wood 0 and Wright 6, and also ran out Nichols with a stunning piece of fielding. Nichols played the ball into the covers and with no fielder there Learie raced after the ball, picked it up and with only one stump to aim at he hit it. England finished on 352 with Learie taking 5–75 in 17 overs.

On day two, Grant's batsmen had one of their best days knocking up 395–6 after a thunderstorm interrupted play for an hour. Jeff Stollmeyer racked up 59, and his elder brother Victor Humphrey Stollmeyer (1916–1999), playing in his only Test, showed his class in scoring 96. The emergence of the three Ws stopped him playing more Tests but he remained a prolific scorer in regional cricket. 'Bam Bam' Weekes followed up with a slam-bang 137 in 135 minutes but the most dynamic innings came from the flailing bat of Learie. He played some extraordinary strokes – one over the head of wicketkeeper Arthur Wood and his great admirer Plum Warner wrote in his column: 'he cut, he drove, he made the most amazing hooks. He also made a few snicks over and through the slips. It was an innings with a strong blend of Jessop in it combined with a preponderance of Constantine himself.' C.B. Fry, another writing cricketer, described him as 'an Indian rubber man with double joints.'

Learie's objective was to reach a first Test hundred but a cross-bat shot against the fast medium bowling of Worcestershire's Reginald Thomas David Perks (1911–1977) was one too many snicks – it carried high to Wood and he walked off with a full house applauding his 79. Tall and broad-shouldered, Perks was clapped in as well for his persevering thirty overs which were rewarded with five wickets for 156. With a lead of 146 there was no chance of a West Indies victory and Hutton, 165* and Hammond, 138, boosted their averages and Hammond declared on 366–3 to save any more energy being expended by the exhausted bowlers. It was a worthy, sporting outcome: the West Indies had proved they deserved true Test status at last.

Wisden summed up saying: 'It was a real joy to watch the carefree cricket of the West Indies on the last day. Constantine, in the mood suggesting his work in Saturday afternoon League cricket, brought a welcome air of gaiety to the Test arena. He revolutionised all recognised features of cricket and, surpassing Bradman in his amazing stroke play, he was absolutely impudent in his aggressive treatment of bowling shared by Nichols and Perks. While the four remaining wickets fell those two bowlers delivered 92 balls from which Constantine made 78 runs out of 103. Seldom can there have been such a spreadeagled field with no slip, and Hammond did not dare risk further trouble by changing his attack. With an astonishing stroke off the back foot Constantine thumped Perks for six to the Vauxhall End – a very long carry – and helped himself to 11 fours before he was last out to a very fine catch by Wood, running towards the pavilion the wicketkeeper held the ball that had gone over his head.' Another cricket writer described the scene: 'a glorious hour of roman candle, rocket and giant crackers. It was Constantine's Test match.'

Learie had played in almost every match – to meet the team's requirement to fill seats in the ground to guarantee that the tour turned out to be profitable – and on the eve of his last Test appearance he disappeared. He went off to the country for a walk, stopped to eat his sandwiches and have a soft drink and read a book before returning to the team hotel later in the day. Rolph Grant was furious, quite rightly. Learie wrote: 'When I returned in the evening I was given a terrific trouncing by the skipper. I told him it was time I took a little interest in my figures in a Test match. If I failed in this one I was prepared to take the criticism.' His mistake was to ask for a day of rest. It is a moot point whether one of today's stars – like Ben Stokes – would be treated in a similar fashion. Would he have been left out of the side in similar circumstances? Probably not. Perhaps fined. Learie wasn't punished.

One story about him concerns appealing in an unsporting manner. He was batting for Nelson in his last season against Todmorden when their talkative wicketkeeper Tommy Carrick appealed loudly for lbw. The bowler Fred Root wasn't so keen on appealing and Learie turned to Carrick and shouted, 'Not out!' like a mad dervish. At the end of the over Carrick said to Fred, 'He's feared me Freddie. I don't fancy appealing again. I thought he was going to bite me.' Fred said, 'He won't hurt you. It's only his excessive keenness.' Next over Carrick appealed again and Learie reacted the same way, shouting in a loud voice, 'Not out!' Carrick pointed to the umpire and shouted back to Learie saying in his Lancastrian accent, 'Thee shurrrup. I'm not asking thee, I'm asking t' umpire!'

Hubert Preston, the *Wisden* editor and father of Norman, who later filled the post, wrote an inspiring epitaph for Learie's finale: 'He repeated all the amazing energy that made him one of the most dazzling cover points when he was first came to England. No matter where placed, he performed wonders on getting to the ball. In bowling he stood out by himself. He was the most unflagging member of this very alert side. His batting reached a climax of audacious adventure in the Oval Test when he often electrified onlookers with his impudent zest for runs.'

Learie bowled more overs than anyone on the tour and his 103 wickets cost the low return of 17.77 and earned seventh position in the first-class bowling averages of the year. His 614 runs were below what he anticipated – his batting average was a mere 21.17 – but he played most of the more explosive innings.

He was voted one of *Wisden*'s 'Five Cricketers of the Year' in the 1940 *Almanack*. The other four were Bill Edrich, Walter Keeton, Brian Sellers and Doug Wright. None of them had the star appeal of Learie. He was the first West Indian to be honoured and the article finished by saying: 'he will never be forgotten.' A copy of the tribute contained a major error: he was called Leary! In his book *Connie: The Marvellous Learie Constantine*, Harry Pearson used the word 'bunt' in describing a shot which means 'stopping the ball (like in baseball)'. Learie rarely bunted. His objective was to hit the ball as hard as he could. In that 1939 tour Headley was the batting icon with 1,745 runs, average of 72.70, backed up by Jeff Stollmeyer and Weekes. The class came from Headley and the Stollmeyers and Learie and Weekes were the anti-bunters.

People who knew cricket and loved it readily acknowledged Learie's immense contribution to the then national game. Denis Howell, Britain's first sports minister, watched him in a match at Edgbaston in his youth and said, 'It was a spiritual uplifting.' Denzil Batchelor, the writer and author, said, 'He was the incarnation of revolutionary cricket.' Sir Hilary McDonald Beckles, the West Indian academic, said, 'He was the first truly great West Indian.' Noel Wild of the Nelson Leader wrote, 'There was no more electrifying cricketer in the game. He had an effervescence both on the field and off it that was thrilling and infectious.' Michael Manley, former prime minister of Jamaica, said, 'He was one of the greatest personalities in the game.' Sir Dingle Mackintosh Foot QC (1905–1978), Liberal and Labour MP, Solicitor General in the Harold Wilson years who died choking on a chicken sandwich in Hong Kong, said, 'I never met anyone who inspired more widespread affection among all sorts of people.'

Micky Stewart, OBE, one of England's greatest fielders, particularly at short leg, once said, 'Learie taught me how to field. In my teens I used to take the tube to St. John's Wood and watch one-day matches at Lord's on a Saturday and I marvelled at his fielding prowess even though he was nearing fifty. When I got home we used to go to local parks and set up games and I copied how he did it. When I was picked for England and met him he used to say 'in our day' as though I was the same age as him although he was thirty years older than me. I looked on him as a hero. He had a peculiar bowling action. As he was about to release the ball his arm shot up high into the air like pulling the alarm on a train. He was quick in his younger days and gave it a good old whack with the bat.'

Most outstanding West Indian cricketers who were knighted in recognition of their superstar status, including Gary Sobers, Wes Hall, Viv Richards, Curtly Ambrose and Everton Weekes agree that the Caribbean has produced its last cricketing all-time great. Brian Lara was the last. T20 has eroded its Test standards and the West Indies is in danger of being an also-ran, lacking of class.

The Oval Test finished on August 22nd, two weeks before WW2 started. Six more matches were scheduled but they were all cancelled. Barrage balloons – designed to try to stop low-flying Luftwaffe aircraft bombing London – were being put high around Parliament and the Oval and people were being encouraged to stick sticking plaster on their windows to minimise the breaking of glass if their property was attacked. A total of 1,750 barrage balloons were used, a third of them around London, and 102 German aircraft were downed in the Blitz.

It was no time to play cricket. Some players wanted to stay on, especially because they wanted to play Ireland in Dublin before sailing off from Liverpool to America. Others wanted to catch the first boat available. If Grant and the other players had agreed on the earliest departure – minus Learie and Martindale who were going to their homes in Lancashire – they could have booked their tickets for the 13,580-ton liner SS *Athenia* departing Liverpool, which was sunk on September 3rd by U-30, one of the first fourteen U-boats to leave Germany two weeks earlier.

Instead, they boarded the SS *Montrose* at Greenock, having caught a night train from London on September 1st. The ship called in at Liverpool to pick up 800 passengers and a few hours later, another 400 at Greenock joined the packed vessel. The cricketers, like the other passengers, were alarmed about their chances of survival, knowing that 118 died when the *Athenia* went down. Two days out in the Atlantic a message came from the Admiralty advising the captain of the *Montrose* to return to Greenock. The U-boat was still in the vicinity. Six hours later, the all-clear was sounded and the journey started again. It was completed safely.

The *Athenia* was the first vessel to be sunk in WW2. At 16.30 hours, only a few hours after Britain declared war, the Oberleutenant Fritz Julius Lemp spotted a large ship 250 miles NW of Ireland, about sixty miles off Rockall, a barren sixty-three-foot rock sticking out of the sea. Lemp gave the order to dive and get a closer look. The *Athenia* was travelling at maximum speed, zigzagging and giving the impression it was a warship, not a liner. He sent his crew to battle stations and they fired three torpedoes. The first one hit the *Athenia* in midship and the second and third both malfunctioned. Lemp heard a distress call from the vessel and realised he had broken the Prize Regulations which Germany signed up for in 1936. Under the agreement, merchant ships had to be searched and if carrying contraband, they were sunk after the crew had evacuated to lifeboats. Attacks on liners were strictly prohibited.

It was twelve hours before *Athenia* finally went down, on the following morning. There were 1,100 passengers including women and children and 311 were Americans. Three merchants ships and three British destroyers soon arrived to pick up the survivors. Most of the 118 who perished were drowned when the Norwegian rescue ship *Knut Nelson* crashed into lifeboats.

Joseph Goebbels, the German Propaganda Minister, claimed the British had sunk the *Athenia*. Nations around the world condemned the inhumane sinking of the liner. On May 7th, 1915 a German submarine sunk the SS *Lusitania* eleven miles off Old Head of Kinsale, Ireland, killing 1,198 people including many Americans. There were 761 survivors. But the *Lusitania* was carrying fifty tons of armaments. The case of the *Athenia* was different. There was no contraband or armaments being stored below deck. Hitler was furious because Lemp had made a ghastly mistake. By the time Lemp had sunk two other ships and destroyed two British aircraft, he was forgiven and looked on as a hero.

TEN

EXCHANGING CRICKET BALLS WITH SANDBAGS

Safely home in Nelson, Learie was pondering his future. His studies for becoming a lawyer continued but he needed a job to pay the bills. Windhill Cricket Club from the Bradford League offered him a contract after his less memorable season at Rochdale in 1938 but once the War began they reduced the offer realising that the club might struggle by losing their players and also spectators. He could have returned to the safety of Trinidad but hardly gave a thought to the idea. 'This is my home in Nelson and I feel I owed this country a lot,' he said. 'If I had gone to Trinidad I would have felt like a rat leaving a sinking ship.' Within days of his arrival the Council offered him a job as an ARP, an Air Raid Precautions observer dealing with the possibility of Luftwaffe air raids. Around this time the cotton industry was collapsing in Lancashire and many of the fourteen mills in Nelson switched to other means of production or were demolished. In thirteen nearby towns factories were adapted to shell-making, which made them targets. Happily Nelson hadn't joined in.

As a precaution, Learie, Norma and Gloria moved into one large bedroom at 3, Meredith Street. He explained, 'If a bomb fell on the room, we all went. If it hit the other room, we might be lucky.' Bombs landed half a mile away, dropped by a German bomber which was supposed to attack Liverpool Docks. Learie's first task was to fill sandbags and place them around Reedyford Hospital along with a gang of mainly volunteers.

He was also appointed a billeting officer, looking after families who were evacuated from Manchester and Bradford, both cities having been under aerial attack. In a broadcast some years later, he said, 'I never knew until then the extent of the slums and of poverty. It would do many of my own countrymen good to see and appreciate this for themselves.' For almost half the year deprived people lived in tiny, squalid houses with little or no proper heating unlike Trindadians who rarely experienced temperatures under 60°F.

Nelson's most eminent resident was welcomed in every house he inspected, somewhat different to when he first arrived in 1929. This time he was looked on as a black messiah, a man to be respected. He observed, 'I never knew the extent of poverty until I arrived in the town.' He hadn't been called up for military service but was expecting it. While waiting for the summons, he applied to the Ministry of Labour in Manchester for a more senior job. A letter arrived, asking him to attend a medical to assess his fitness for the army in Blackburn. Though a number of famous sportsmen used excuses to avoid being called up, Learie was not one of them. Before he set off, he received a telegram from the Blackburn Employment Exchange saying, 'Do not take medical: report to the Employment Exchange here instead.' After a brief interview with one of their officers, he was offered a job as a civil servant in the welfare department of the North West division of the Ministry with responsibility for West Indian migrants on Merseyside and also West African seamen now living in Liverpool.

He had a small clerical staff under him and his number two was Sam Morris, who later became Deputy Chief Officer of the Community Relations staff. Morris proved to be the ideal person to help the cause. Learie commuted from Nelson but often stayed at Colwell House where the migrants first stayed before accommodation was found for them. Many of them were poorly educated and were reluctant to work. They had no training before having to work long shifts in factories to manufacture shells. Some companies refused to take black men and if they were forced to, didn't pay the same wages as to white workers. Learie had to persuade the unions to allow the migrants to join, to enable his recruits to receive the same wages.

He recalled, 'You couldn't believe the difficulties I had working with my own people. They grumbled, complained about their digs. And we had to do almost everything for them as you would for children – remittances to families at home, questions of what to wear and so on.' He told them he was an ordinary man like themselves. Their resentment about the way they were treated was slowly replaced with admiration. Most of them had heard of Learie and they were cricket lovers back home. They relished his stories about playing against the finest cricketers of the time like Bradman, Hobbs, Larwood and many more.

One of his admirers was Bessie Braddock, the Labour MP for Liverpool Exchange, who had a reputation for plain talking. She said of him, 'He used all the tact in the world and common sense as well.'

Christened Elizabeth Margaret Bamber (1899–1970), she changed her name to Bessie when she started out as a young member of the Independent Labour Party and married a Jock Braddock. Her father descended into alcoholism and the family lived in Liverpool with one of the highest mortality rates in the United Kingdom. There were three Elizabeths in the ILP group and they drew lots for new names to differentiate from each other – Elizabeth, Liz and Bessie – and she drew the more distinctive name of Bessie. A heavyweight of fifteen stone, she was also nicknamed 'Battling Bessie' because of her forceful approach calling for change in one of the most deprived parts of Britain. Her favourite sport was boxing. A teetotaller and a non-smoker, she was the first woman to be suspended in the House of Commons in 1952 for continuing to protest when the Speaker told her to sit down and stop talking. In WW2 she served in the Liverpool ambulance service as a driver. There were sixty-eight bombing raids on Merseyside and on May 1st, 1942 fourteen ambulance drivers lost their lives. Harold Wilson delivered the address at her funeral in 1970 and he said, 'She was born to fight for the people of the docks, of the slums, of the factories and in every part of the city where people needed help.' There is a statue of her outside Lime Street Station, Liverpool's main railway station.

Bessie had lots of meetings with Learie during the War and they never fell out. His keen sense of humour helped to solve many of the problems, assisted by her Scouse humour. He was never confrontational. He would start with a smile and the person who was complaining realised that he wasn't dealing with a tyrant but a genuinely nice man who was willing to take time to sort things out. The 2017 December edition of *The Cricketer* contained a picture of Learie looking back from his desk and in front there were three trays. They were labelled 'IN', 'OUT' and 'LBW' (which stood for 'let the buggers wait'). One person he wouldn't keep waiting – the honourable Bessie Braddock. One of Bessie's favourite boxers was James J. Braddock (1905–1974) who won the world heavyweight championship in 1935, beating the German Max Baer, and who held the title for just two years. Descended from Ireland stock, the 'Cinderella Man' was born in Hell's Kitchen in the dockland of New York, a similar background to Bessie.

A lot of West Indians were traditionally known as womanisers and many of the problems concerned fathering children and abandoning the white mothers on Merseyside. US soldiers, black and white, also helped to bring children into the world whose fathers weren't staying long before being drafted to war zones. Not many took an interest in seeing the children grow up. Learie began trying to raise money to support the mothers – through holding cricket matches featuring well-known cricketers and appeals, until he found it was too burdensome: it was the job of the local social services, not his.

He encountered an ugly incident in a dance hall when an American Air Force officer shouted, 'Get out, we don't allow niggers to mix with white people.' Learie politely told him to go away. The officer screamed, 'Get out, nigger, before I smash you.' In one of his books, Learie said, 'He added a coarseness which really roused me, for I was talking to a husband and wife and another girl who probably didn't often hear those words. I had marked the spot where I should strike him with a formidable blow. But walking the length of that hall cooled me. I became aware of the newspaper headlines that would have resulted and the general inflammation of the black and white problem which it would cause, with England at that time filled with black and white American troops. So, rather sadly, I handed him over to the porter at the door and the troublemaker was told to leave. Later, the place was put out of bounds for all US troops.'

Around 20,000 West Indians came to Liverpool, London and Cardiff, working mainly in munitions factories. Ninety per cent of the war material carried by ships from the USA docked in Liverpool and nearby and the eleven miles of quays were constantly bombed by the Luftwaffe. Starting in May 1940 until January 1941, Merseyside was the second heaviest place to be bombed next to London. Learie's office was close to St. Luke's church, which was partially destroyed. A bomb killed twenty-two inmates in Walton Jail and the most appalling incident was when 365 died in a large shelter three days before Christmas Day. Liverpool Cathedral was hit and the biggest bang came from a high explosive bomb which landed on the SS *Malandal*, docked in Huskisson Dock, where its cargo of 1,000 bombs hadn't been unloaded. The explosion obliterated several docks yet only a handful of people died. Ironically, a bomb destroyed a house in which Alois Hitler, half brother of Adolf, used to live.

Doubtless the Reich leader would have continued the Blitz on the cities of Britain but he was secretly building up a vast armoury to take on Joseph Stalin's Red Army. Operation Dynamo, the codename of the evacuation of the British and French forces from Dunkirk, took place between May 26th and June 4th, with 334,000 British and allied troops transported across the English Channel to safety. On June 22nd Operation Barbarossa began the German invasion of Russia. Hitler had lost interest in trying to capture Britain.

Over the years Learie knew and assisted some of the 492 passengers and stowaways, mainly from Jamaica, who arrived on 22nd June 1948 at Tilbury in the *Empire Windrush*, a former German-built steamship previously named MV *Monte Rosa*, which transported German troops and Norwegian Jews in WW2. They disembarked close to where Elizabeth I once delivered a Churchillian-style speech to her forces and later watched the English fleet routing the Spanish Armada in 1588. She said she was only a weak woman but would lay down her life to prevent her nation being occupied by infidels and claimed she had the heart and stomach of a king. The well-wrapped West Indian families on the vessel needed those qualities.

The word 'Windrush' – named after a tributary of the river Thames in the Cotswolds – has gone down in infamy in the history of the last days of the British Empire. Seventy years later Mrs Theresa May, the Conservative premier wrestling with problems of Brexit, had to make an abject apology about the way most black immigrants were treated, along with a penitent then Home Secretary Amber Rudd. The MP at Hastings and Rye had to fend off determined efforts in a Home Office Select Committee hearing which lasted two days at the end of April in 2018. She just managed to keep her post after admitting she misled Parliament about a secret report about targets. But on the Monday she resigned.

Mrs Rudd went to Cheltenham Ladies College, which produced well-brought-up young ladies, and married the writer A.A. Gill before the marriage was dissolved in 1995. One of her credits was her brief appearance in the film *Four Weddings and a Funeral*. The name Amber – probably the first British Cabinet minister to bear that name – originated in the late nineteenth century, taken from gemstones and derived from Arabic. It became popular after the film *Forever Amber*, first shown in 1944, written by Kathleen Windsor. A Labour MP made a pert remark after she resigned saying, 'She was too long on amber and needed the red!'

With losing so many soldiers in the war and women anxious to return to normal family life there was an acute shortage of labour in the late 1940s. So Clement Attlee's government brought in the British Nationality Act in 1948 giving the right of citizens living in the Caribbean islands to be considered as British and they weren't subject to immigration restrictions.

The *Monte Rosa*, battered by Allied aircraft and submarines, was taken over as a war prize when the fighting ended and renamed. In the summer of 1948 it transported demobbed West Indians serving in the British forces back to their islands and an astute officer of the owners placed an advertisement in a Jamaican newspaper asking young men if they wanted to go back to England and take a permanent job. Those who accepted the offer were known as the 'Windrush Generation.' Their arrival wasn't well received by the white majority. Not all were virtuous. In Liverpool during the war Learie dealt with a number of cases of desertion and its problems of single-parent families.

The *Windrush*'s last journey came in 1954 at the end of the Korean War transporting British troops back to the UK. James Weymouth, a *Daily Telegraph* reader, had a letter published in the newspaper in 2018 which said, 'Our family boarded in Hong Kong and in the early morning of March 28th, 1954, thirty miles off, an explosion in the engine room caused a fire that quickly swept through the ship. Within the hour it was abandoned; women and children took to lifeboats and most of the men, including my father, had to take their chances in the sea. Four of the 222 crew died but all 1,276 passengers were saved. It was considered a miracle that there were not more deaths and injuries. The ship sank next day.'

Another *Daily Telegraph* reader, Tim West of Matlock, pointed out that *Windrush* wasn't the first post-war Jamaican voyage to England with migrants, saying, 'The first was my father's ship, the HMT *Ormonde* in 1947 when it docked at the Albert Dock in Liverpool. *Ormonde* was returning Caribbean solders and was advertised in the *Sunday Gleaner* for passengers wanting to travel to Britain on the return. This was to be at their own cost; 108 people applied.' One wonders whether the 108 people were disqualified as British subjects and told to go back to their place of birth.

In 1971 the Immigration Act granted the migrants an indefinite stay and most of them didn't have any evidence of being bona fide British. In 2010 the Home Office destroyed their landing cards and three years later in a purge on reducing the flow of migration, they were ruled non granta – 'persons not appreciated' – and were told to go. Mrs May was Home Secretary at the time and with the support of the Cabinet in 2012 she confirmed only those who were considered legal migrants. The Home Office was seen to create a hostile environment for illegal migration. Her underlings mistook that to mean removing the survivors from the *Windrush* expedition who hadn't kept their arrival documents and their children. When the howls of protest reached the House of Commons, the Conservative government did a swift U-turn, awarding the victims compensation. Learie would be one of the first to join the revolt. He could have assumed a Nelson Mandela peace-making role had he lived.

Each June 22nd Britain's honours the Windrush Generation. Speaking at the seventieth anniversary, Lord Bourne the Communities Minister said, 'It recognises and honours the enormous contribution helping the country rebuild as well as their descendants. The day will be supported by a panel of British-Caribbean representatives who will offer £500,000 every year to distribute to local communities and charities – 'to keep their legacy alive for future generations, ensuring that we all celebrate the diversity of Britain's history.' A national service of thanksgiving was held in Westminster Abbey on June 22nd, 2018 to commemorate the anniversary. Sadiq Khan, the Mayor of London whose family migrated from Pakistan, pledged to do the right thing and said, 'It could be my mum, my brother, my uncle or even me.' Significantly, he told the Commons Home Affairs Select Committee that only sixty-three members of the Windrush Generation may have been wrongly deported.

Someone who influenced Learie greatly was Dr Harold Arundel Moody, born in Kingston, Jamaica in 1882, who migrated to London in 1911. Both men were moderately left of centre and believed fervently that equality should apply in all countries, not merely with countries dominated by white people. Moody's writings, partly influenced by C.L.R. James, won support from educated people throughout the British Empire and he launched the League of Coloured Peoples in

1931. Membership shot up. Moody wasn't an activist organising campaigns in the streets. He was a gentle persuader and Learie was similar.

In March 1943 he persuaded the League to hold their first annual meeting outside of London. Gerald Howat wrote: 'The week was spent discussing wartime problems of coloured people with special reference to Merseyside. Constantine, after only a few months in office, gave a picture of conditions which was cautiously optimistic. Others gave him the credit for the smoothness with which so many West Indians had been absorbed into the community. A few months later the League produced his Charter calling for self-government in the Caribbean and ending discrimination in jobs, in places of public entertainment, restaurants and other public places.'

Learie acted as a spokesman and found himself being invited to speak at meetings, schools, youth clubs, churches, hospitals and in local government. He was one of the first sportsmen to appear on BBC's Brains Trust explaining the problems with being a black man living amidst a white population. A feature writer from the *Daily Herald* said, 'His personality, common sense and idealism was an outstanding feature of an excellent discussion.' The BBC retained him as a spokesman for the oppressed and he worked as a freelance for many years, eventually becoming a governor of the BBC. He won support wherever he went. He was invited to comment on cricket for the BBC and local radio stations as well and soon became authoritative with his views and his Trinidadian lilt appealed to most listeners.

A correspondent of the *Scotsman* wrote, 'In a rich, musical voice, the speaker told, without a word of bitterness, of the treatment he and his family had received in different parts of England in a period of years on account of colour. It was calculated to evoke shame or sympathy in equal measure.' He was particularly good at visiting wounded West Indian soldiers, aircraftmen and seamen in hospitals. Many of them lost arms and legs and he would say, 'I have been lucky, I haven't lost limbs but I have gone through the world with a drawback almost as bad, the drawback of a black skin.'

Moody died in 1947 with his work still undone and Learie took over as president for a while. Another doctor, Hastings Banda, later President of Malawi, played a prominent part in running the organisation. Two prominent Labour ministers who assisted Learie were Ernest Bevin (1881–1954) and George Tomlinson (1890–1952). The heavyweight Bevin was Minister of Labour in WW2 after becoming a founder and general secretary general of the Transport and General Workers' Union. He was born in a small village called Winsford in Somerset and was illegitimate. He left school at twelve, almost illiterate, and rose to become Foreign Minister in Clement Attlee's Labour government. The other one was George Tomlinson, a son of a cotton weaver and he also left school at twelve and worked in a cotton mill. He was Bevin's Permanent Secretary and was a conscientious objector in WWI. With their connections, it was not a surprise that Learie was honoured in the 1946 New Year's Honours List when he was awarded the MBE for his community service in the North West of England.

Howat thought Learie was suspicious of one group – the Anglican clergy. The then Bishop of Liverpool, Albert David, was indifferent, he said and added, 'He treated me courteously but only apparently because he was obliged to do so as a matter of business. I thought the Anglicans were inflexible with regard to colour segregation. Like many men who gain a reputation for usefulness in the colour problem all he appeared to want from it was the ability to segregate white and coloured, and to want to keep the coloured people sufficiently fed and clothed and housed perhaps, but definitely kept "in their place."' David Sheppard, the Sussex and England batsman who was Bishop of Liverpool from 1975 until 1997, was the opposite. I knew him well and he played cricket against black people for most of his cricketing career and they respected him. When he died in 2005, he was recognised as one of the most humane and understanding of senior clerics in England.

Much of Learie's work concerned helping Africans, as well as West Indians, who manned vessels bringing goods to Liverpool Docks. They were looked on as an underclass and were often left without a ship, with hardly any money. One of their leaders, Ekarte, led a strike and Learie managed to win concessions from the bosses. Ekarte rewarded him by kissing on both cheeks. In those days a vast majority of men never kissed each other but in the modern world – particularly in football, cricket and other sports as well as in politics – it is becoming commonplace.

Learie also did lectures to Army, Navy and RAF personnel. One of his biographers, Undine Giuseppi, a Barbadian married to an Italian who was Principal of the University School in Trinidad, wrote: 'His zeal and enthusiasm for the task in hand never faltered. To his numerous admirers, therefore, it came as no surprise when in recognition of his services he received the MBE from King George VI in 1946. Much as he appreciated this honour, he took even greater pride in the illuminated scroll he had received from the men with whom he had worked and whose cause he had championed during those strenuous and at times heartbreaking years.'

Professor Giuseppe claimed WW2 proved almost a death blow to the game of cricket. Learie soon proved her wrong. His deep passion about the game stayed with him throughout his life. He seized every opportunity to play and in 1939–1941 he was the highest paid cricketer in the Bradford League appearing in the Windhill Cricket Club. But she was right about one respect: the War heralded the end of Learie's elongated eighteen Test career. He played in thirteen Tests against England in which he scored 569 runs in 23 innings with a highest score of 90 and five wickets against Australia, the top two countries in international cricket between 1928 and 1939. His tally of 72 runs in 10 innings was modest against Australia.

He bowled 578.3 overs, 125 of which were maidens, and captured 58 wickets at roughly three a Test for an average of 30.01. His batting average was 19.24, modest for an all-rounder, and a figure often criticised. Even the harshest critics wouldn't carp about his total of 28 catches, 2.1 per Test. His standing in that department is unchallenged, alongside the South Africans Colin Bland, Jonty Rhodes and Abraham Benjamin De Villiers, known as AB. Today's list of the Top Ten Fielders contains names from the post T20 era, ignoring Learie. It is a shame that little film of him was taken in his prime otherwise he would still be figuring high in the list. Had he faced Zimbabwe, Bangladesh, Sri Lanka or even New Zealand, his statistics would have been much better. As Professor Giuseppi said, 'No cricket figures can truly reflect his greatness.'

Windhill, a hilly area of the same name in Bradford, was only twenty-two miles from Nelson and Learie often took his family to watch his last club in action at weekends. The club, founded in 1863, was moved to a new ground in 1923 in Busy Lane paid for by the proceeds from a bazaar, which raised £459. Windhill CC was looked on as a nursery for talent going on to play for Yorkshire, the then most successful county. It was also an equivalent to Nelson in the Lancashire League and they had won the Bradford League title in 1937, 1938 and 1939 and when Learie joined them in 1940 he helped his new club to make it four titles in a row. He scored a modest number of 366 runs, including a century against Brighouse inside an hour and took 76 wickets at 11.80 including a hat-trick – at the age of thirty-nine. He was chosen to represent the Bradford League against a Yorkshire XI team captained by Herbert Sutcliffe to raise money for the Red Cross. A crowd of 7,000 boosted the funds to a sum of £380, at the Park Avenue ground. He didn't disappoint the crowd, lashing another century in an hour with 74 from boundaries.

The match was a declaration game – surprisingly – and Bradford League called a halt on 259–7 and Sutcliffe's less explosive response was 127 in his side's 209–6 with the match left as a draw. It was one of the first major charity matches of the War, which he starred in, and it a set a pattern, similar to what Stan Matthews did later in the War and afterwards. Early on in these series of matches Learie was paid his expenses and a fee. Later, when he become an amateur, he appeared without reward.

In August 1942 the two League representative sides met again and Learie made just six and took 2–13 in another draw. Sam Morris, his deputy in the welfare department in Liverpool said, 'I went to see him in a Saturday charity match. The grounds of the little Lancashire town were packed to capacity. Needless to say, the crowd came to see this fabulous West Indian cricketer. He prepared to receive the first ball. He did and that was the only ball he faced. Clean bowled for a duck. The look of incredulity on the face of the bowler was shattering. One could sense his sorrow at what he, or rather the ball, had done and one felt that he wished the cricket laws could be bent to allow Learie to have another go. There was a momentary hush among the crowd and he continued to walk back to the pavilion less than two minutes after he had left it. The ovation he received was greater than the reception he had going in to bat. This spontaneous ovation was not for cricketing achievement on that day at least, but for the tremendous all-round reputation he had already built up in this country.'

Learie managed to squeeze in another championship season in 1941 giving Windhill, with a population 1,410, five in succession and he became only the second player in the Bradford League to take four wickets in four balls against Lidget Green. He had to leave the club then, through pressure of work, but returned to play at the end of the War for several seasons while in his late forties. Besides Learie and his close friend Manny Martindale, a number of cricketing stars played for Windhill including Charlie Parker, Johnny Lawrence, the Somerset leg-spin bowler who taught Geoff Boycott to be a Test great, the Derbyshire pair Alf Pope and Bill Copson, Ellis 'Puss' Achong, Syd Buller, Les Ames, Lou Vincent, the former New Zealand batsman who was convicted for fixing matches and Ajmal Shahzad, one of the first players with an ethnic background to play for Yorkshire and England.

In 2016 the Windhill committee was forced to resign from the Bradford League because of a lack of players and resources. David Young, the League chairman, said, 'This is extremely sad and with the season approaching, they had no scorers, helpers and ground personnel as well as a limited playing squad. Nobody likes to see the demise of a cricket club and we will do all we can to encourage former players, officials and supporters to offer assistance to try and ensure that the name of Windhill doesn't disappear from the cricketing landscape.'

Despite having more projection than ever today – cricket is shown on TV from all parts of the world particularly in Britain, the people who started it all off – and with more coverage of newspaper, radio and social media given to the sport, the number of clubs in Britain has fallen. Fewer and fewer state pupils are taking up the game because only 7% of schools – public schools – actively support cricket. Sunday cricket played by villages and amateur clubs is diminishing rapidly and Learie, had he been alive, would have been horrified. Another Learie, or a Denis Compton or a Gary Sobers, is needed to bring about a revival of interest – genuine heroes, not T20 fakes.

Learie played a prominent part in arranging an all-West Indian team to face an England side to raise large sums for the war effort. One of the first matches took place in August 1940 at Lord's when Pelham Warner brought along Len Hutton and Denis Compton, the biggest names in English cricket at the time. Two of Learie's close friends in the West Indian side were Dr Bertie Clarke and the West Indian barrister and broadcaster Ernest Clarke. I knew both men. They were men of stature, wonderful ambassadors for the cause of equality in an unequal society in Britain. Bertie starred with the ball, taking 5–68 and Ernest scored 47. Ernest often did summaries with the BBC sitting alongside John Arlott, and later, Jim Swanton at Tests. Denis Compton won the man of the match award, scoring 73 and surprising the large crowd by taking three cheap wickets with his Chinamen.

Three years later another match featured Learie's West Indian side against a much stronger England XI watched by an almost full house at Lord's. Alec Bedser bowled out Learie's side for 120 with figures of 6–27. His fast, nagging medium swing bowling later took his total in fifty-one Tests to 236 wickets after the War and missing six years while serving in the RAF, when he was in his prime, cost him many more wickets. He was evacuated from Dunkirk with his twin Eric – they were born within ten minutes of each other – and they went everywhere together. They even shared a bank account, lived in the same house and never married. Alec turned down the chance of being a Flight Sergeant because he wanted to stay with the same unit as his brother. Eric died first, aged eighty-seven, and Alec, with his strong physique which enabled him to bowl in 35°C temperatures in Australia without a break, survived four more years. The only time he came close to going off the field Down Under was when he felt ill in a Test in Adelaide, went to the boundary and vomited. He wiped his face and walked back to the middle and resumed bowling. Christopher Martin-Jenkins said of him, 'The ethics and hard work and clean living have never had a sterner champion.' England won by eight wickets and with the crowd wanting more, MCC laid on a match. Learie entertained the crowd with two massive sixes off Doug Wright in his 59 scored in forty-five minutes.

Pelham Warner played a key part organising cricket at Lord's, taking up the job of deputy assistant secretary. The RAF moved in to use the buildings and the Nursery Ground but the playing area and the stands were available for matches. Another succession of ad hoc elevens, mainly involved with the services, raised sides for charity with the proceeds being devoted to the war effort. The matches were one innings each, completed in one day. There was no limit for overs and most of them ended in draws. The British Empire XI used a number of English county players and Bertie Clarke was a regular with Learie making odd appearances. Warner believed the main purpose, next to raising funds, was to raise the morale of both the players and the spectators.

The fear was being bombed. Manchester United's Old Trafford was hit by bombs, also the cricketing Old Trafford ground a five-minute walk away. A bomb landed on the Lancashire CCC's members' dining room, another was dropped on the groundsman's quarters and some stands were damaged. The county decided to close its Old Trafford ground until the War ended. It was used by troops evacuated from Dunkirk and other troops who were in transit coming and going from theatres around the world. German POWs helped restore the ground for the resumption of cricket in 1945. The Oval was requisitioned by the Army ready to receive Germans parachutists but none was sent there: instead it was turned into an ack-ack and searchlight fortified centre. Luckily it wasn't bombed.

On three nights between December 22nd and Christmas in 1940, 250 aircraft dropped 470 tonnes of high explosive and 30,000 incendiary bombs, which virtually destroyed much of the centre and east of Manchester. The targets were the factories which built most of the RAF bomber aircraft around the city except that indiscriminate bombing carried on relentlessly elsewhere. The cathedral, built in the early fifteenth century, was a sufferer but the Grade II Edwardian Baroque Midland Hotel, built in 1903 at a cost of £1m, where touring international cricket teams stayed and which Learie knew well, was unscathed. The rumour went – probably started by Lord Haw Haw who broadcast nightly from Berlin to Britain during the early part of the War – that Hitler ordered Hermann Goering, head of the Luftwaffe, to avoid bombing it. Hitler was reputed to have said that when the Germans eventually occupied England, he admired the building so much he wanted it as a GHQ in the North West. Lord Haw Haw – William Brooke Joyce, an Anglo-American (1906–1946) – was sentenced to death for treason and hung at Wandsworth Prison after the War ended.

The Christmas Blitz left around 650 people dead, more than 2,000 injured and 50,000 houses damaged. The indomitable spirit of their then population of 700,000 enabled the Mancunians to carry on with the Christmas festivities, as best they could. St. John's Wood was relatively missed by German airmen. In 1941 a bomb hit Lord's and there were no casualties and little damage was caused. MCC consulted with the authorities and were told to carry on playing, in a restricted manner. The only other scare took place in July 1944 when during a match between the Army and the RAF, a V-1 doodlebug – the flying unmanned bomb known as the Vengeance Weapon – dropped nearby. The players were warned to throw themselves to the ground and when it exploded, causing minimal damage, the match resumed. The facing batsman, Middlesex's Jack Robertson, struck the next ball for six. In just under three months close to the end of the War,

9,421 V-1s were fired from Europe and there were 7,000 deaths, mainly in London and the Southern counties.

Learie appeared in a Dominions side against an England XI on August 2nd–3rd in 1943 including Australians, New Zealanders, South Africans and fellow West Indians Manny Martindale and Bertie Clarke. Fourteen thousand spectators enjoyed the sunshine and the high scoring, mainly by the home side. On the second day the Dominions were set 360 runs in two sessions. Instead of playing for a draw, opener Charles 'Stewie' Dempster, one of New Zealand's finest openers who was never coached, scorched along to 113, Clarke hit up a speedy half-century and Learie's brisk, brief innings ended on 21 when Leslie Harry Compton (1912–1984), leaning back against a fence on the boundary, caught the ball and claimed the catch. With no TV cameras, only the long tom cameras of a couple of photographers, there was no technological assistance and the umpire raised the finger. A spectator shouted, 'No, it was over the line. It was a six.' But Learie 'walked,' and was rapturously clapped in to the pavilion.

Both the Compton brothers were sportsmen of the highest order and Denis, in particular, 'walked' when he was out. He started out as a slow left-arm Chinaman bowler who could bowl the googly and batted number eleven for Middlesex in 1936. His brilliance and unorthodoxy with the bat soon brought a top order position and for the next twenty-eight years he lorded it over England's best batsmen until his 'Compton knee' finished his distinguished career. Leslie was a wicketkeeper but in the Dominions side he was considered an adopted West Indian. He was never capped by England's cricket selectors but made two appearances for the England football team. He made his debut at the age of thirty-eight and sixty-four days, a record which still stands. Suffering from diabetes, he had a foot amputated two years before he died in 1984.

Besides carrying out his onerous work on Merseyside Learie made the tiring train journey from Nelson to London to take part in charity matches. Now approaching forty-five, he was still eager to continue but his body was slowing down. He became bulkier making it more difficult to propel the ball at speed. His innings were shorter but often, even more explosive. In the field his reactions were no longer quicker than anyone else in the side. The last England XI versus a West Indian side, usually arranged by the efficient Bertie Clarke, took place in 1945. Learie, with 32, was the top scorer in the West Indies' meagre 84. It led to a crushing defeat.

His most enjoyable wartime matches were for the British Empire XI and Clarke was one of the major organisers. They played 238 matches using overseas servicemen and others on leave and they raised £20,000 for various war charities. Learie played in eight games. His best score was 63, made in as many minutes and he took 15 wickets at 14 apiece. The Victory Test in August at Lord's was one of his proudest moments and it was labelled a first-class fixture. It was his final first-class game. Lindsay Hassett was the Dominion skipper but on the eve of the match he was taken ill and dropped out. Pelham Warner, the Dominion manager, was faced with a dilemma. He wanted to give the honour to the only non-white player, Learie, but there were younger, fitter candidates. Warner, always the gentleman, came into the away dressing room at Lord's and asked for a consensus about the captaincy. There was a unanimous Aye vote – Learie.

Wisden described the three-day match 'one of the greatest games ever produced.' Lord's was almost packed for the three days and the Dominion side won by 45 with eight minutes remaining. There were 1,241 runs scored with an average of 413 per day – a kiss of life for the ailing game of cricket as the War ended. New Zealand's left-hand opener, Martin Paterson Donnelly (1917–1999), known as 'Squid' because of lack of inches, dominated the first innings of the Dominions with an elegant 133 in a total of 307. Neville Cardus called him 'the finest left hander of the age.' A major in one of the Tank regiments, his twin brother Maurice died in the 1918 flu epidemic and he played in only seven Tests. He preferred going to Oxford University and broadening his approach to life.

England's legspinner Doug Wright, 5–90, and the Australian Cec Pepper, also a leg-spinner and a sledger, responded with 4–54 to dismiss England for 287. Walter Hammond was at his most masterful in his innings of 121. Learie bowled the second most number of overs in England's knock – 15–2–53–1. Highly commendable for a forty-four-year old! Keith Ross Miller (1919–2004) had opened the innings and told Learie, 'My back is crocked, take me off,' after his first over. So it was a surprise to find 'Nuggett' Miller coming in at second wicket down spearheading the Dominions' counterattack with an astounding 185 in 165 minutes, with six sixes.

No sport has had a more flamboyant, errant and dismissive of normal customs performer than 'Nuggett.' If he hadn't been one of the greatest all-rounders he probably would have been cashiered when he flew Mosquitos in the Australian RAF. He had a number of near-death incidents including crashes, spurned orders from superiors and though he gave the impression he couldn't care less about anything, his teammates and aircrew loved him. He was the Errol Flynn of cricket. Errol played for Sir Aubrey Smith's Hollywood CC in Los Angeles – badly – in his heyday and was known for being late, often inebriated and accompanied by a host of potential starlets. 'Nuggett' had a number of mistresses both in Australia and England and once he admitted that two rich ones who lived in the King's Road were mother and daughter, performing in the same bed. When he met my wife Audrey he used to chat her up. 'I've heard of your reputation,' she always laughed.

A highlight in my low level cricket career was facing him in the nets at Old Trafford when he worked for the *Daily Express* after he retired. I wasn't wearing a box, a chest protector or a helmet when he walked up, picked up a ball and shouted, 'You ready?' He was standing a couple of yards from the bowling crease. I expected a half-paced delivery, or even an off-spinner. But he charged forward, his right, high arm whizzed over and a bouncer reared up towards my head. Fortunately I didn't have time to duck and kept my eye on the ball and swayed backwards to avoid it. He laughed. 'That's enough. I can see you can bat a bit.' And walked off. He was famous in his prime when he occasionally stopped walking back to his mark, turned and bowled at the same, fast pace. It was difficult to judge the speed but it must have been 80mph plus. He was born at a place called Sunshine, in Victoria, and he brought sunshine to his life and everyone else's until his cancer caught up with him at the age of eighty-four.

At Lord's 'Nuggett' put on 117 in forty-five minutes with Learie, 40, for the sixth wicket and that was the decisive stand in the all-out total of 336. England had to make 330 in two sessions. Hammond, with 102, completed the fourth century of the match and Doug Wright snapped up another five wickets for 105. Seventeen wickets were taken by two leg-spinners. For true cricket lovers it felt like being in paradise.

Pepper (1916–1993) had seven victims in the match, hapless victims of his immense range of deliveries. He had similarities to 'Nuggett' in personality. He never stopped talking, particularly in the middle and some people, including Don Bradman, took offence with his barbed comments. He was good enough to play for Australia for a long time but Bradman and his friends made sure he wasn't picked. He appealed for two lbws against Bradman in a Sheffield Shield game and when the umpire rejected them, he accused Bradman of cheating. Instead, he settled in

England, playing League cricket and between 1954–1980. He was a respected umpire in English cricket. Peppery was a good description of him. He had pungent words about everyone and when asked if Ian Botham was the best all-rounder of his time, he said: 'Botham? The world's best all-rounder? Hell, he wouldn't have got into the New South Wales dressing-room in my day. I could have bowled him out with a cabbage, with the outside leaves on.'

Learie's final contribution in his last first-class match came from a flash of brilliance when he ran out Eddie Phillipson. He wrote about it: 'How I longed for that moment for youth again and the lightning in my right hand. I should have loved to put myself on to bowl and try one or two scorchers. But I had not the pace and I had to think of something else quickly. I spoke to a bowler and asked him to bowl a few bait balls to encourage the batsmen to take liberties to wide mid on. With the last one the batsmen were on the move for another run and I picked the ball 30 yards from the wicket, my hand swooped as in my youth and I saw Phillipson's stumps jump all into the air.' It was a good way to go. As he took the plaudits he said, 'I'm proud to be able to lead you in. I'm "colony" while the rest of you are "Dominion."' He was the only black person in the epic game.

Some of his most enjoyable freelance cricketing engagements around this period were played in Scotland. In September in 1944 he captained the All Blacks which contained black players from Sierra Leone, the Gold Coast (now Ghana), Nigeria as well as from the Caribbean. They lost by 25 runs to an Anglo-Scottish side. One of his favourite places was Kilmarnock, population 46,000, where Johnny Walker whisky came from and it produced two Nobel Prize winners from a state school – Alexander Fleming (1881–1955), the inventor of penicillin and John Boyd-Orr (1881–1971) for his work on nutrition – also William Wallace, the fourteenth-century rebel leader and sports writer Hugh McIlvanney who died in January, 2018 at eighty-four. The biggest crowd to watch a cricket match at the town's cricket ground, at the time, saw his Combined side beat another Services side. Next day he took six for 23 at Troon. After these matches he gave talks.

In the following year he visited Scotland again, appearing in four successive matches in as many days. It was a punishing schedule and instead of pacing himself, he agreed to play ten successive days cricket for Major H.B. Rowan's XI against schools. Every day he coached the boys before going on to the field. Despite his tiredness, he managed to make an entertaining unbeaten 67 at Trinity College in Glenalmond in Perth, probably the most beautiful ground in Scotland. One pupil said of his innings, 'It was like magic.'

ELEVEN

'WE WON'T HAVE NIGGERS IN THIS HOTEL!'

On July 30, 1943, Learie, accompanied by Norma and Gloria, who was aged fifteen, arrived at the Imperial Hotel in Russell Square with their luggage and Learie's cricket bag for the England v Dominions match at Lord's starting on August 2nd. They weren't greeted with a smile, more of a scowl. The hotel, situated on the east side of the square and built between 1909 and 1911, was full… only of white people, mostly American soldiers. Learie rang in advance to book a family room and having been turned away from a hotel in Brighton in the past, he mentioned his family was black. The booking clerk raised no objection and carried on writing down the details. The booking was confirmed. Learie had sent a cheque for £2 as a deposit.

The Constantines were given their room key and went to their room. Shortly afterwards a porter knocked at the door and said the manager wanted to speak to Learie at the reception desk. Arnold Watson, a colleague of Learie working with the Ministry of Labour in Liverpool, had arrived and someone had remarked that there were guests unhappy to see 'niggers' staying in the hotel. When Learie heard that he was incensed, naturally. Margaret O'Sullivan, the manageress, arrived and asked him to leave next day and bring his bags down because the door would be locked to prevent his family returning to the room. She offered him an alternative room at the next door Bedford Hotel, owned by the same company that ran the Imperial Hotel. Watson tried to persuade Ms O'Sullivan to change her mind. He told her Learie was a British passport holder and a respected civil servant working for the government.

Ms O'Sullivan refused, insisting that the American officers had strict rules about segregation. At the time the US military segregated black soldiers from white ones and that lasted until 1948 when the US Government Executive Order 9981 was signed. But some form of segregation continued until after the Korean War (1950–1953) when 36,516 Americans died and 128,650 were wounded. Watson said Learie was captaining the Dominion cricket team at Lord's who were serving in the forces and it was an honour to have a West Indian in charge.

Ms O'Sullivan, with a raised voice, said, 'You can stop tonight but not any longer. You can go when you like. I can turn you out when you like.' Norma and Gloria were upset and tempers were further heightened when the manageress told Watson, 'We are not going to have these niggers in our hotel.' When Watson asked Ms O'Sullivan why she replied, 'Because of the Americans.' She said she feared an ugly scene which would soon get out of hand. The police might be called and the staff wouldn't be able to handle the situation.

Finally Learie and his family, still fuming, accepted the offer of a room at the other hotel. Next day they moved to the Bedford Hotel, named after the Duke of Bedford and their heirs who owned Russell Square. Except for the row about Learie's eviction Russell Square was looked on as a peaceful place but in 2005 two terrorist bombs exploded nearby killing fifty-two people of sixteen nationalities of different colours. In 2016 a mental patient Zakaria Bulhan attacked six people there and one female died.

Learie had met Paul Robeson (1898–1976), the great American singer and social activist, and he knew all about the story of him being asked to leave the dining room at the Savoy in 1930 because his presence upset the white clientele. Robeson lived in a house in Hampstead at the time and appeared in several musical hits on the London stage and also topped the bill in a Royal Command Performance. As a handsome man who was chased by women admirers, he left his wife and had a relationship with fellow star Peggy Ashcroft before returning to his wife. Martin Luther King had the same weakness. After WW2 Joe McCarthy (1908–1957), the infamous Wisconsin Senator, waged vicious attacks on what he called communist sympathisers in the entertainment business and one of his targets was Robeson, whose career went downhill afterwards. But his persistent agitation for equal rights continued until he died.

The first use of the N word was in 1574 but the first usage in a dictionary in England was in 1795. It came from the negroid heritage of black people of Africa and the noun originated from Spanish-Portuguese meaning black. It was picked up by John Rolfe in 1619 when he called the slaves who were transported to Virginia, USA 'negars'. The slave owners looked down on their slaves as inferior, uneducated people and more than half died on the voyages to the Caribbean.

By 1900 there was a nationwide campaign in the USA calling for the word 'coloured' to be used in place of black and in the early 1960s the Civil Rights Movement emerged to convince the majority of the population that change was needed. Martin Luther King set if off with his impelling, heartfelt 'I have a dream' speech delivered in front of 250,000 people in front of the

Lincoln Memorial in Washington on August 28, 1963. Hundred of academics voted it the best speech of the twentieth century in 1999 and one said, 'It put it up against the ones of Lincoln and Jefferson which shaped the history of this nation.'

The cause was helped by Cassius Clay, later known as Muhammad Ali (1942–2016), who used the N word when he refused to be called up for the Vietnam War. Between 1967–1970 he was prevented from defending his titles until his suspension was lifted. Up to then the N word was as looked on as a slur or an insult.

Now it is elevated to 'a racist crime.' On January 20th, 2018, most of the Premier League and Championship clubs staged a one-minute silence for Cyrille Regis (1959–2018) the popular England and WBA and Coventry black footballer. He didn't actively campaign for the elimination of racist comments on the football field but his example was held up as a token to encourage today's young people. Cyrille, born in French Guiana, rarely lost his temper when someone baited him and usually laughed.

Learie had lots of influential friends and he used his contacts to start legal redress in the courts about his humiliation at the Imperial Hotel. The newspapers picked up the story but with newsprint in short supply, the coverage was meagre. One close friend was Sir Dingle Foot, later the Solicitor General of the Harold Wilson government and an MP who was a Liberal before becoming a Labour MP. Learie studied in his law chambers for a while. Another was Ernest Bevin, the Labour Foreign Minister.

A month later an MP planted a question in the House of Commons about Learie's predicament. There was no law at the time about discrimination against black people and Ernest Bevin rose to express support for Learie. The case was heard in the King's Bench Division in the High Court on June 28th–30th in 1944 in front of Justice Norman Birkett (1883–1962), later the first Baron Birkett. He was born in Ulverston, then in Lancashire, a son of a draper, who went to school in Barrow-in-Furness Grammar School and graduated at Emmanuel College, Cambridge. Founded in 1584, it is one of the wealthiest colleges in the world and one of the few possessing a swimming pool. Females were admitted in 1979 and same-sex marriages were introduced in 2006. Norman followed his father as a Methodist preacher and soon won a reputation as one of the outstanding public speakers of the day. One of my clubs, the Forty Club, voted his speech at their dinner the best in the club's history. He didn't play much cricket but was well versed in it. He became a Liberal MP and in 1945 he was an alternate judge in the Nuremburg Trials.

A high-powered legal team was recruited to represent Learie. The senior counsel was Sir Patrick Gardiner Hastings (1880–1952), born in London, son of a bankrupted solicitor who went to school at Charterhouse where he was often bullied. In 1924 he became Solicitor General in the Labour government. He, too, was an MP, representing Wallsend, Lancashire. Several of his cases involved Sir Oswald Mosley, the leader of the Fascist Black Shirts. Dame Rose Heilbron (1914–2009) was Learie's junior counsel and she was the first woman to become a QC. Daughter of a Jewish hotelier, born in Liverpool, she was a pioneer for the women's rights in what had previously been a male preserve.

By coincidence Learie had been back at Lord's captaining a Dominions XI against an England XI in a one-day match on June 10th. Ernest Bevin was sitting in the Grandstand along with the Colonial Secretary and his friends Ernest Eytle and Bertie Clarke came in at three and four with Learie coming in at five. The Dominion side caved in, all out 77, and to keep a big crowd entertained they batted a second time after Walter Hammond scored 106. They failed to reach England's total but in the final ten minutes Learie top-scored with 42, which included a six and eight fours. 'It took me back to 1928,' he said.

The High Court case was brought on the basis of an alleged

breach of contract by the company owning the hotel. Their defence was that although it had refused the Constantines' accommodation, he had left voluntarily and it had performed its obligation in common law by putting him and his family at the Bedford Hotel and they were happy to stay there. Justice Birkett knocked down that idea, dismissing it by saying, 'Of no matter,' and added the company had enough rooms to receive the Constantines. He said, 'Constantine was a man of high character and although he was a man of colour, no ground existed on which the defendants were entitled to receive and lodge him at the hotel. He behaved in his evidence with modesty and dignity at the time of the incident and in the courtroom, where his evidence was generally regarded as erudite and impressive. A traveller is, in my opinion, entitled to choose the hotel at which he desires to be a guest, and the defenders are not entitled to put a traveller, desiring to use their hotel, to the trouble and expense of finding another hotel.'

Justice Birkett criticised the conduct of Ms O'Sullivan who denied that she used the word 'niggers' and he called it 'deeply offensive.' There were enough witnesses who heard it. In today's rush to litigation there would be substantial claims for damages. Anything to do with racism or inappropriate sexual behaviour is brought before the courts and large sums are paid out. Learie behaved in a gentlemanly manner: he was satisfied not to be compensated. Justice Birkett ruled, 'It only remains for me to say that I was urged by counsel for the plaintiff to award exemplary damages or substantial damages in this because of the circumstances in which the denial of the right took place when the plaintiff suffered, said as he did suffer, much unjustifiable humiliation and distress. I do not feel upon the authorities that I can accede to the submission and request, having regard to the exact nature of this action and the form in which it comes before me. My conclusion upon the whole matter is that I must give judgment for the plaintiff for nominal damages and I, therefore, award him in this action the sum of five guineas (five pounds, twenty five pence).' That would be about £60 in today's more moderate inflation.

Learie explained his reasoning – 'Had I been inclined to ask for damages I would probably have succeeded in a further action for defamation. But I was content to have drawn the particular nature of the affront before the wider judgment of the British people in the hope that its sense of fair play might help protect the people of my colour in England in future. From the tone of the hundreds of letters of congratulation I received from all over the country, I think my object was attained.' He may have won magnificent victories on the cricket field – not as many as he should because the West Indies only played against England and Australia in his time – but being on the winning side in the High Court was his greatest achievement to date and it paved the way for a Race Relations Act. He was the man who broke the colour bar. Unfortunately it took twenty-one years to put it on the statute book.

In 1954 he wrote a book called simply *Colour Bar*. He wanted it to be called *Black and White* but the publisher thought *Colour Bar* would make a bigger impact. It sold reasonably well and it gave impetus to the campaign for an Act of Parliament. He began the book by copying out the Universal Declaration of Human Rights and talked about the experiences of a black cricketer in the United Kingdom. The Declaration of thirty articles was approved by the United Nations in Paris in December 1948 and Eleanor Roosevelt, wife of US President Franklin Roosevelt, was one of the authors. It was based on the four freedoms laid down by FDR – the freedom of speech, freedom of religion, freedom from fear and freedom of want. There were sixty-eight member countries and forty-eight voted Yes, none voted No and eight abstained: the Soviet block, Saudi Arabia and South Africa. The Declaration didn't come into effect until 1976. Learie wrote in his book, 'If it had been brought in at once, I wouldn't have written my book.'

In the aftermath of the High Court action a naval officer and his wife offered to share his flat in London, and he wrote to a lady in Kent saying 'I want to assure you that it has left no bitterness whatever and I am not likely to judge the kind people I have met, and many others, by the attitude of such people. I apologise for being so tardy in replying but you will understand that the volume of correspondence has been tremendous.' He had hundreds of letters of congratulation and he tried to answer every one. David Low, the brilliant *Evening Standard* cartoonist, penned a thought-provoking cartoon about contrasting the way Learie was treated in a nation which was fighting for freedom to protect people of all colour against a racist hate-filled Nazi country.

The Bedford Hotel now charges about £160 a night, the same as the Imperial. As though the owners felt some guilt, the Imperial was rebuilt in 1966. They have yet to put up a Blue Plaque to commemorate Learie's action ending discrimination in the United Kingdom. But he has two plaques – the one in Meredith Street in Nelson and another one at the flat he lived in at Lexham Gardens in Kensington from 1949. Years later I had an amazing coincidence when I learned Learie's Blue Badge in Lexham Gardens was only a six hit from the Cromwell Hospital where Audrey died on Christmas Day 2000. My children and I stayed at the now demolished Derby Hotel opposite the hospital and we could have inspected it. On it says "West Indian cricketer and statesman lived here 1949-1954."

Too old to play any more first-class cricket, he earned a considerable amount of money from playing charity matches and coaching in Scotland, Ireland and Sri Lanka. His freelance broadcasting with the BBC blossomed but his legal studies to qualify as a barrister lagged and Norma had to prompt him, insisting that he was in danger of failing his varied and difficult examinations. Later in 1944 he was admitted to the Honourable Society of the Middle Temple, giving him access to the best lawyers in the country. And many of them were cricket fans. Doors were opening for him.

Roman Law was a stumbling block for him, also Latin, which he had to learn in his late forties. Norma geed him up, saying, 'I locked him in his bedroom several hours a day. I knew that he wasn't getting on with his studies as he should be, with so many callers to the house. If I hadn't taken action we both knew that he would never become a barrister.' After three dedicated years of study, he eventually passed in Roman Law. He was on his way.

Playing for Windhill CC gave him a new cricketing lease of life. 'I couldn't have kept going year after year in competitive cricket but the charity games gave me the cricket I wanted without the pressures.' In a BBC programme he was asked about his future and he said, 'Now my job is coming to the end. My future is obscure. At one time cricket was my religion. It gave me a chance of a decent life. It brought me publicity and a wide range of travel. It gave me, as well, reasonable scope to educate Gloria. Now I am older and cannot maintain my standard of bowling fast, catching almost everything that came my way and making runs at the rate of two per minute, a change was needed. I must give up something. Cricket was a way of life. I want to complete my legal studies and if successful, then take a decision. I would love to work for my people. Work in the field of education and self-government for the colonies. This opens up a wide range of probabilities and for the moment confuses me.' As Gerald Howard observed, 'He'd reached a mid-life crisis.'

He captained Windhill in 1946 and with George Dawkes, who made his debut for Leicestershire at sixteen and set a number of records for Derbyshire's wicketkeeper, and Manny Martindale, who took 56 wickets at 9.80, succeeded to transform the side.

He was the leading bowler in 1947 and also 1948. His 45 wickets at 10.48 in 1948 played an important part in them becoming champions. In a Priestley Cup game against Queensbury he scored 101 with eight sixes and ten fours. In his final game against Keighley at his home ground he dismissed four batsmen and with the last ball of the match he hit a boundary to finish unbeaten on 69. He said, 'I had to do something to mark the occasion and despite fine and steady bowling, I won the game with a final four which went humming to the boundary as clean as any ball I have ever hit.'

On Mondays he flew to Dublin from Manchester to coach Trinity College, Leinster CC and St. Mary's College and the members of staff were highly impressed with his way of putting over his ideas. Father Francis Berry, master of St. Mary's where Learie coached the boys in the lunch hour, said, 'He was really a fantastic coach. Every moment of the hour was used at the nets and no boy was idle. There was perfect discipline and the boys learned a lot of things. It bore fruit in the subsequent years in our winning all the inter-school competitions and giving a great boost to the game which we still in some way feel thirty years later.'

During a visit to the south of Ireland Learie met the Irish president Eamonn de Valera and the President shared his views about equality for black people. Not many black people lived in Ireland in the 1940s. There was a glitch afterwards when a photograph was taken of them together and Learie paid for a print that was promised to be sent to his home. It never arrived. He suspected that someone had vetoed the idea for some unknown reason. More visits were made to play for the Colonial CC in Edinburgh and H.B. Rowan's team in 1946 to pass on his cricketing expertise to students. One official, Jock McCurdie, said, 'Nothing is left to chance. His precision was outstanding. He even tells you what time you are going to bed and what time to get up. Not one, not even a lazy fellow, is a minute late for anything.' England's Ashes losing team in 2017–8 ought to have had a Constantine as manager! In 1953 he accepted an invitation to coach in Sri Lanka from the prime minister Sir John Kotelawala for three months, accompanied by Norma. It was a welcome, relaxed trip to a beautiful island which he said was 'full of nice, smiling people who loved cricket.'

Learie's habit of making long-time friends helped him to start out as a cricket commentator. After play in his wartime matches at Lord's he was invited to join the commentary team and did a stint for the West Indian radio stations. And the man who changed his life as a broadcaster was Rex Alston. Born in Faringdon, Berkshire, and son of the Bishop of Middleton, he was born in 1901 and christened Arthur Reginald Alston. He didn't like the name of Reginald and changed it to Rex. An all-round sportsman – he was a rugby Blue at Cambridge, captain of Bedfordshire Minor Counties, and an athlete who competed with the sprinter Harold Abrahams – he made his debut with the newly created *Test Match Special* on July 25th, 1946 at the England v India Test. Rex was universally popular, what today would have been termed 'old-school', with his charming manners and wonderful voice. Sitting next to Learie, he dispensed good habits in front of the microphone and years later Learie said, 'I cannot fully express how much I owe to his help generally.'

In 1985 Rex collapsed and was taken to Westminster Hospital at the age of eighty-four and a couple of days later *The Times* mistakenly published an obituary of him. A man with a great sense of humour, he treated it as a joke when he recovered and he remarried Joan Wilson, his second wife. He had a ready quip when he met anyone – 'I'm the only person who married a year after *The Times* reported my death.'

This was a golden age for cricket commentators. Leslie Thomas John Arlott, OBE (1914–1991), with his distinctive Hampshire burr was joined by C.B. Fry, Brian Johnston, CBE,

MC (1912–1994) and E.W. Jim Swanton, OBE (1907–2000) of the *Daily Telegraph*. Arlott, a policeman, a poet and a writer, who claimed he made one first-class appearance for Hampshire, as a substitute fielder, was from the far left wing but 'Johnners' and Swanton were on the far right wing and their off-mike exchanges in the studio should have been recorded for posterity but weren't. I knew them all and they were men who were loved for their wit and strong views. 'Johnners' was a wicketkeeper for Eton 2nd XI and his father, Lt Col Charles Johnston, DSO, MC, drowned at the age of forty-four at Bude in 1922 and 'Johnners' also had a distinguished military career. He landed in Normandy three weeks after D-Day and took part in the battle of Arnhem and was awarded the MC for rescuing tanks under fire.

Ernest William Swanton also had a chequered military background. He was captured by the Japanese at the fall of Singapore and spent three years as a POW working along the Burma-Siam railway. As an officer he didn't do all the hardest work but lost an enormous amount of weight. He managed to save a 1939 copy of the *Wisden Almanack* which he lent to others, particularly Australians, to goad them by reading reports of England's Ashes series the year before. Meeting these doyens of cricket commentators must have broadened Learie's mind and increased his knowledge. All of them lasted a long time at the top of their profession. They didn't need to have been Test cricketers, which seems to be only the requirement in today's media.

A veteran cricket lover from Southampton wrote to him after the Test match against India and said, 'I feel compelled to write and tell you how much I enjoyed listening to your commentaries. Your voice is so quiet, so cultural, in fact attractive, too. I am now too old to sit on a hazel bench or to stand so I have to be content to listen.' Another fan wrote, 'I have never in my life listened to such an illuminating and impromptu running commentary.'

Two good friends of Learie did most of the coverage

from the West Indian angle. Alva Clarke, a St. Lucian, did the broadcasting and Jimmy Cozier, father of Tony Cozier, the editor of the *Barbados Advocate*, wrote for the Caribbean newspapers. Alva said of Learie: 'He could speak without a script and was a superb broadcaster, a producer's dream.' John Arlott said, 'His approach was simple and direct. He never embarked on involved constructions. He was an extremely good, natural broadcaster who adequately expressed the shape of a cricket match.'

Learie reported on the 1950 series when the rejuvenated West Indies side, boasting the three Ws, won three to England's one Test. Former Jamaican Prime Minister Michael Manley summed it up: 'To the Caribbean the victory was more than a sporting success. It was proof that a people was coming of age. They had bested the masters at their own game on their home turf. They had done so with good nature, with style, often with humour but with conclusive effectiveness. Allan Rae, Jeff Stollmeyer, Frank Worrell, Weekes and Walcott made hundreds to the delight of thousands and to establish the foundations upon which victory was to rest. The victory itself was procured by "those little pals of mine, Ramadhin and Valentine."

'When the Lord's Test was played the wave of migration from the West Indies was to come. Smaller in number, the Caribbean fans were less confident and hence, less noisy. As a result when Lord Kitchener led a happy, chanting, hip-swinging, black Caribbean celebration round the hallowed turf at Lord's the procession was more impressive for its enthusiasm than its size.'

The West Indies bowled 1,115.5 overs in the series and took 77 wickets and the twenty-two-year-old tiny Trinidadian Sonny Ramadhin, the 'mystery' off-spinner, and the tall, willowy slow left arm spinner with the long fingers, Alf Valentine, bowled 790.2 overs – 69% of the overs and took 70% of the wickets. Sonny took 26 wickets at 23.23 and Val 33 at 20.42: an incredible feat by two unknowns outside the Caribbean.

In the following years Learie was invited to take part in various BBC programmes including *Women's Hour*, schools broadcasts, *Children's Hour*, *Commonwealth Club*, *London Forum*, *Radio Roundabout*, *West Indian Diary*, *The World Goes By* and music quizzes. These talks brought in extra income to make up for not having continued as a professional cricketer.

One of his weak points was making trivial factual mistakes. In one programme he named the wrong hotel in the High Court action and the programme director had to reprimand him. Gerald Howat reckoned he could be long-winded. But he added 'although errors might abound, fluency prevailed.'

Sometimes he had to turn down offers to give talks because he needed to spend more time on studying for his legal exams. In 1949 he decided to move to London. The tenancy of their house in Meredith Street in Nelson ran out and in mid summer they rented a flat at 101 Lexham Gardens, off the Earl's Court Road. Gloria had graduated at St. Andrew's University as a Master of Arts to go to the Institute of London University. Another reason was because the best tutorials for the bar examinations were in London.

In 1950 he passed Constitutional Law and Legal Education and Criminal Law. A year went by and he passed Contract and Tort and Land Law. More success came but the strain of the extra costs he had to pay, and his growing weariness left him feeling slightly depressed. C.L.R. James asked him, 'Are you thinking of giving up?' Learie retorted, in Churchillian defiance, 'Who? Me? Not on your life! Same on the cricket field. Absolutely the same.'

TWELVE

TIME TO GET DOWN TO WORK

Learie had made a considerable amount of money from League cricket in the 1930s and in his mid forties he was still playing in charity matches but his income had suffered and now it was time to get a proper job, like qualifying as a barrister, a task which proved to be difficult for him. Progress was slow and Norma continued to be a kind of mentor, urging him to sit down quietly and study the dry law books. Gerald Howat's interview with her revealed how tough she became. She told him he had to study Latin and Learie told a friend, 'She made me learn the declensions and conjugations and irregular principal parts.' Howat said, 'Norma kept his nose to the grindstone.'

Playing cricket at the highest level and speaking in pubic brought him into contact with many important people in all kinds of professions and his gift of making friends easily opened many doors. His enlightened West Indian friends shared his belief that Great Britain should give independence to the Caribbean region, Trinidad and Tobago, Jamaica, British Guiana and later, the smaller islands. Politics began to take over his cricket.

Moving to Lexham Gardens, off the busy Earl's Court Road, was a prime area for him – close to the BBC at White City where he performed his frequent broadcasts, the embassies of various countries and dependencies and an easy underground ride to the Inns of Court. In 1950–54 he sweated through the Part 1 and 2 examinations of law. No one gave him grants. He paid for his admissions, call fees and for his lectures himself. It was a hard slog. Finally in 1954, aged fifty-three, he emerged as a fully qualified barrister. The *Nelson Leader* headlined their story 'Local Boy Makes Good.'

At the same time he served on the Colonial Office Advisory Committee on racial matters. One of his friends, Seretse Goitsebeng Maphiri Khama (1921–1980), known as King of Bamangwato, also trained to become a barrister at the Temple Chambers and the political row which followed when Seretse married a white woman, Ruth Williams (1921–2002), a typist at Lloyd's, in 1948 propelled Learie into the headlines. The governments of Britain and South Africa, Seretse's tribe and millions of people in the old Empire were opposed to a black tribal King marrying a white woman. Learie saw it as an example where the colour bar needed to be lifted. He was engaged writing his book of the same title and this was a time for him to speak out. His views roused opposition from many quarters, especially from Oswald Ernald Mosley (1896–1980), the 6th Baronet of Ancoats, MP, leader of the British Union of Fascists and his son Max who was still in the news, for the wrong reasons, in 2018. Oswald's hectoring voice, reminiscent of Adolf Hitler and Benito Mussolini, persuaded many bigots to join him and despite being imprisoned between 1940–3 as a threat to national safety he was exiled to Paris. But he was still allowed to visit London occasionally to rant to a dwindling number of adherents.

The Church of England refused permission for Seretse and Ruth to be married in their churches and they had to marry in a registry office. The name Seretse meant 'the clay that binds' – very apt. The Oxford University educated Seretse became King at the age of four when his father died and his uncle Tshekedi Khama, who assumed titular power, objected and the couple, now living in Serowe, the capital of Bechuanaland, were forced to return to England. Bechuanaland was the third poorest country in the world with only 12km of made-up road at the time and was a protectorate of Britain. The Labour government of Clement Attlee was in the middle of an economic crisis at the time and set up an inquiry about the affair. Their decision was to tell the couple not to return but for his unfortunate marriage. Thirty years later, the findings, held up through the Official Secrets Act, did not contain those words.

Learie became chairman of the Seretse Khama Fighting Committee and meetings were held throughout the country. Learie was not just speaking to black people but to educated, decent white people as well. Members of Parliament of all parties wanted to take some action but nothing happened. Learie was one of millions who blamed South Africa's apartheid white government. The British government owed almost $4 billion dollars to repay to the US after WW2 under the Marshall Plan and relied heavily on South Africa's gold and uranium. Labour's Tony Benn and others took up the cause of Seretse but Attlee told him he couldn't change his mind because his government needed cheap gold to meet the repayments to the US Treasury.

Eventually Seretse and his wife went back home in 1951 as private citizens after his renouncing the tribal throne and started a cattle farm, unsuccessfully. He set about setting up a Democratic Party and his popularity won enough support of his tribesmen to vote in his more acceptable government. Suddenly everything changed. Reforms were brought in and he knew that diamonds had been discovered and insisted the profit went to his tribe. In 1966, Seretse, now president, was able to declare independence from Britain. Corruption was brought to an end and investment from other countries followed. Seretse won three elections in succession before he died at the age of fifty-nine from cancer of the pancreas. In 2008 one of his sons became president. Seretse proved to be one of the finest leaders in the tangled history of Africa. Ruth and their five children remained. In 2016 a film about the story of a black king and a white typist entitled 'A United Kingdom' was given a good reception but it wasn't a moneymaker. It cost $14m and drew just $13.4m from all around the world, most of the money coming from USA and Canada.

The Seretse affair was one of Learie's outstanding accomplishments because eventually good prevailed over bad. His fierce opposition to apartheid remained throughout his life. In normal circumstances, he would have loved watching and commenting on the England v South Africa Test series in 1965 in the *Daily Sketch* but he told his readers 'it would be on my conscience if I stayed for the series'. In the next year Her Majesty the Queen Elizabeth appointed Seretse a Knight Commander of the British Empire.

Around this time Learie was asked to stand as a Liberal candidate in Shipley, near Bradford, and his friends in the Labour Party including Bessie Braddock, Ernest Bevin and Herbert Morrison urged him to accept. He declined and said he wasn't keen to join the Labour Party either. He met Clement Attlee (1883–1967) several times and thought he wasn't sympathetic to the black influx of people from the West Indies. A son of a solicitor and seventh child of a family of eight and born in Putney, Attlee was educated at Haileybury College, an expensive public school, and gained a second-class degree in Modern History at Oxford. Shipley is now controlled by the Green Party. Jim Laker, another of Learie's friends, was born at Frizinghall, part of the borough of Shipley. A road is named after him there,

Jim Laker Place. I was Jim's ghostwriter when he was signed by the *Daily Sketch* before Learie was recruited.

With more television sets being sold in Britain and with Learie appearing on more BBC programmes he was more recognised in the streets and one occasion, when we were walking along Oxford Street to a meeting, a couple coming the other way looked at him and smiled. Learie started up a friendly talk with them and they parted almost friends. That became a regular event. He always had time for strangers.

Colour Bar was reprinted in 1954 and made a considerable impact. Learie wrote that he enjoyed himself in England but his little family of three still encountered discrimination of many forms. On one occasion he and Norma booked two bunks in a four-berth sleeping compartment on a train going to Glasgow for Gloria's graduation at St. Andrew's University and when the other two people turned up they refused to share with them because of colour.

Shortly afterwards his former employers Trinidad Leasehold Ltd contacted him and invited him to become assistant to their legal advisor at an annual salary of £700. Surprisingly, he took little time to accept. He'd lived in England for twenty-five years and he missed the sun in the Caribbean. In the winter months in England he experienced respirational problems in England.

Another deciding factor was Gloria's forthcoming marriage to a lawyer named Andre Joseph Valere, which was imminent in Port of Spain, and Norma had gone there to help the arrangements, leaving Learie to pack their belongings at the Lexham flat ready to migrate back home. Tall and handsome, Andre was a man of easy disposition who was extremely popular in Trinidad and the list of invitees grew and the wedding soon turned out to be one of the biggest that year.

Learie had set sail from the oil tanker *Regent Hawk* from Bristol and landed in Trinidad on December 15th. He met with a rousing welcome. In the company magazine *Regent News* someone wrote, 'seldom has public acclaim been given so ungrudgingly to a son of the soil.' A civic reception for him was arranged in the Town Hall in the capital. He soon discovered that as a senior member of Trinidad Leaseholds Ltd he would move among white circles rather than the people whom he grew up with, mainly descended from Africa. The staff handbook warned him that it was inadvisable to travel on the state-owned railways and buses. The murder rate was one of the highest in the Caribbean and it still is, with 494 murders in the two islands, Trinidad and Tobago, in 2017 compared to the 571 in the UK which has more than twenty times the population of T & T.

The Constantines were allocated a staff bungalow at 3, Immortelle Avenue in Pointe-a-Pierre, 51km south of the capital north of San Fernando which has the island's only oil refinery. Sir Trevor McDonald, the legendary ITN news presenter, was born and bred in San Fernando. If anyone wondered whether the exotically named Immortelle was after the immortal great West Indian all-rounder, the theory can be soon disabused – immortelle is a composite flower of papery texture retaining colour after being dried, often used to adorn graves. One of the world's most famous wildlife trusts of waterfowl is situated there.

One of Learie's friends in his early days was Reynold Dolly, a medical practitioner who went on to become a director of Leaseholds and helped Learie to settle in. A black man, he proved to be a true friend. Another long-time associate in his younger days was Dr Eric Eustace Williams (1911–1981), a pugnacious, political theorist who went on to become the first prime minister of Trinidad between 1961 and 1981 and was known as the Father of the Nation. He died at the young age – by Caribbean standards – of sixty-nine. Ten years younger than Learie, Williams was the son of a minor civil servant Thomas Williams, descended from English stock and his mother Eliza

Boissiere, from a French Creole background. He was educated at the Tranquillity Government School in Port of Spain – the word 'tranquillity' didn't match his temperament! – and he managed to raise enough money to study at the St. Catherine's College in Oxford where he gained first-class honours in history. He was helped by a donation of £50 from a local politician otherwise he wouldn't have succeeded.

He earned his doctorate with a thesis presenting a convincing case for the abolition of slavery in the Caribbean. He insisted it came from economic reasons rather than humanitarian reasons. In 1939 he studied at Howard University in Washington and his fervent lectures won him a place on the Caribbean Commission through which the US, Britain, France and Holland helped the economic development of the Caribbean. His aggressive approach upset the other members and he was told to leave. He returned to Trinidad and set out to become a political figure with an ambition to break free from Great Britain.

After a few weeks at Leaseholds, Learie and Norma invited the senior staff, mainly white, for a party at his home and only one white couple turned up. At Nelson, he invited white and black, irrespective of colour, and being offended he wondered whether he made the right decision to leave Britain. He said, 'I didn't see eye to eye with my countrymen on so many things. As far as they were concerned I had been abroad for twenty-five years living it up, while they had been suffering in conditions where the feeling of oppression and an understandable frustration about which so many grumble but took no action.'

Joe Appiah, a barrister from Ghana who married the daughter of Sir Stafford Cripps, the Chancellor of the Exchequer in the Labour government after WW2, was a friend of his and suggested he should live in Africa, where the Constantines originated. Learie never really thought it was an option. Instead Eric Williams and his colleagues approached him about becoming the chairman of the new party and qualifying for a seat in the Trinidad Legislative Council.

C.L.R. James had the same background as Williams and when they were in England they often stayed with the Constantines in Meredith Street in Nelson. Williams insisted on drinking German beer and with none available in Nelson he had to get lifts off Learie to take him twelve miles to a pub at Clitherhoe, which stocked a German brew. C.L.R. shared the same fervent political views of the intellectual Williams – left wing calling for independence from Britain – and Williams launched a new party in Trinidad in 1955 called the People's National Movement (PNM). Learie sought permission to leave his job before accepting a post in the party and consulted his boss, J.B. Christian, the general manager of Trinidad Leaseholds, soon to be Trinidad Texaco Inc. Learie said of him, 'Christian was a Scot, one of the most decent people you could meet anywhere. I said to him I was now being asked to be chairman of a party and he replied, 'Well, there is nothing wrong with that because people like you ought to make a contribution to progress your country and I wouldn't stand in your way. You have my blessing. If you win the vote for the Council, you resign, if you lose, you come back here.'

Learie won the seat for Tunapuna, a municipality mainly consisting of Indians rather than Africans where C.L.R. James and the pianist Winifred Atwell were born. His opponent was the Mayor of Port of Spain named Madura and he squeezed in with 6,622 votes to 6,443, a slim majority of 179. PNM won thirteen of the twenty-four seats, winning 38% of the votes. He emerged as a persuasive voice, and when Williams won the general election in 1956 Learie offered him a ministerial post, as the Minister of Communications, Works and Public Utilities. His crammed portfolio included roads, railways, the meteorological service, water supply, electricity, harbours, airports, street lighting, parking restrictions, bridges and it accounted for half of the government expenditure. Whereas Williams was more of a divisive figure, Learie, with his cricketing popularity, won more general support of both the Indian and black communities. His days were filled but he still played in several charity cricket matches as well as coaching at schools.

He helped draft an ambitious five-year plan to make Trinidad a country which become acceptable to be independent. His other role was to modernise a fledgling political party as chairman. Almost every moment of the day was filled.

Williams didn't share Learie's love of cricket. Instead, he was an above-standard footballer in his youth. In his younger days he had a problem with his hearing, which needed surgery to correct. With his dark glasses, he had a foreboding look: he never matched Learie's wholehearted guffaws. He was a brilliant speaker and the *Trinidad Guardian* said of him, 'he was the apostle of revival and people of all classes, professions, colours, races, flocked to hear him.' In September 1956 his party swept to an overall majority in the Council.

With his added workload Learie often had to get up early, sort out the PNM daily demands, do an eight-hour shift at Leaseholds and then go to political meetings in the evening. There was no doubt that he played a big part in achieving the electoral success. He was a vote catcher. He won the seat in the county of St. George close to where he grew up and according to Gerald Howat he'd bought a property there for his parents. He took a sensible decision to resign his legal job at Leaseholds and moved to a house in Tunapura.

His first speech in the Legislative Council, on November 16th, 1956, was about the poor street lighting in many areas of the country. He criticised drivers who drove too fast and parked indiscriminately. Extra money was urgently needed to improve the lighting and he piloted a Motor Vehicles and Road

Traffic Bill through the Legislative Council to regulate parking and bring in one-way streets. The opposition wanted to defer the Bill but Learie spoke passionately about the urgent need for change. He said, 'Too many don't use their lights. The Bill should go through as fast as possible and we shall endeavour to get it through. If drivers would only consider other users of the roads the problems would become much easier.'

His success was quickly followed by another triumph. On March 22nd, 1957, part of the road in the south of the island collapsed and within several hours he came up with a solution. Just over a year later he was involved in a major row about replacing the two ancient steamers SS *Trinidad* and SS *Tobago* which carried passengers and goods between the two islands. Both were considered to be unseaworthy and another vessel, *The City of Port of Spain*, was chartered to be used after it had an overhaul in Martinique. B.S. Maraj, an opposition member, introduced a No Confidence motion in the Legislature naming Williams as responsible for the crisis arising from the sale of the SS *Trinidad* and SS *Tobago* for £8,000.

Learie defended the prime minister against accusations of swindling the government saying, 'I hope this is the last we shall hear about the two ships because all kinds of imputations and suggestions have been made about them. The suggestion was that there was something dishonest about the *City of Port of Spain* and I want to assure my colleagues that I have a reputation for probity abroad. I have travelled the five continents and I have been respected and looked upon as a man of integrity, a man that is honest and I shall be loath to stand in this Council and have members make insinuations and charges against me without registering a solid word of protest. I hope I am not immodest when I say that many people never knew of the West Indies until they got to know of Constantine and if this is the thanks I am going to get from the country for the service I have rendered abroad, then I hope I will live long enough to regret the day when I entered politics.

'I defy anybody, no matter where he comes from, to point his finger at any minister in this government and prove by witness or by any means he considers proper that the government has been dishonest in any of its dealings. When people read Hansard and find this bankruptcy of thoughts in the Trinidad Legislature and members doing nothing else but maligning ministers, they will wonder what kind of people exist in the West Indies. I want to set the records straight. I resent for myself and for my colleagues any imputations of fraud in any transactions we undertake. Many of us are the worse off for being in politics but it is because we love our country and our people. I hope Hon members opposite would be a little more careful about the way they hurl abuse at people.'

This turned out to be the most significant speech he made in parliament but it also caused more controversy. Some of his colleagues resented his words about 'the service I have rendered abroad.' The back-biting made him think whether he ought to continue and retire to a normal life. The opposing members reckoned Williams had turned out to be a dictator. That was partly true. To get things done to improve the quality of life it needed a decision-maker and not a consensual politician. The British government was now ready to grant independence and in 1958 the federation was inaugurated and included as a member of the United Nations. Port of Spain was chosen as the federal capital. A massive fireworks display was arranged at the Savannah where Learie's cricket flourished in his youth.

The federation needed adroit, well-trained civil servants and that was one of its weaknesses. They didn't have enough. In July 1959 a new constitution was brought in, giving extra powers for the Premier, as Williams was now termed, and his chief ministers.

Learie now had an opportunity to visit England and Australia later in the year as a member of the Commonwealth Parliamentary Association with his expenses paid. The BBC booked him for a number of broadcasts and he spoke about the changes in Trinidad and his belief that eventually people in the Commonwealth will soon be treated as equals, not underlings. In Australia, where he hadn't visited for twenty-eight years, he did a broadcast calling on their government to end their all-white policy. He appealed for quotas for African, Asian and West Indian immigrants.

Learie was back on familiar territory at Trinidad when he watched the MCC side representing England at the ground at Leaseholds where he had given advice about putting in new grass pitches. In the Second Test at Port of Spain he was present when a section of the 30,000 spectators rioted on the third day when left arm spinner Charran Singh (1935–2015), the local player making his debut, was controversially run out for nought at 98–8 in reply to England's 382. The decision review system would have averted most of the missile-throwing that followed, proving the decision was wrong. C.L.R James and his friends agreed that his dismissal wasn't the main reason for the anger of the crowd. They maintained that Frank Worrell, who had finished his university course in England, should have been named as captain of the side, not the white man Gerry Alexander.

One bottle was thrown towards the Governor of Trinidad and was adeptly caught by Learie: only someone of his extraordinary fielding skill would have held it. The English cricket writers blamed alcohol for the bottle throwing, which was partly true, but there were deeper problems in West Indian cricket. Their Cricket Board wanted to continue white dominance over the captaincy whereas Learie and most of his PNM colleagues held the opposite view. At the end of the series, won by England 1–0 after they were victors of the Second Test by a margin of 256 runs, Alexander resigned and Worrell, aged thirty-five, was given the captaincy in the next series in Australia, which ended in triumph for him.

England's captain in the Caribbean, Peter May, was also dismissed for a duck and in his second innings he was caught and bowled for 28 by the hapless Singh, who was promptly dropped. He was picked again in place of Sonny Ramadhin and was omitted for the following Test and that ended his brief Test career. Fred Trueman, who had a habit of calling the home players 'Sunshine,' contributed most to England's victory taking 5–35 in 21 overs on a slow, easy-paced pitch in temperatures in the high thirties. The outspoken Yorkshireman was highly critical of the West Indian umpires E.N. Lee Kow and Sandy Lloyd and called for English officials.

The author of a report for *Wisden* blamed 'the heat, overcrowding, excessive drinking, gambling and disappointment over the batting of Alexander's team.' Learie agreed on all points. West Indies had won the 1950 series in England and they were producing younger, fitter cricketers of class and they included Sir Frank Worrell, Conrad Hunte, Rohan Kanhai, Gary Sobers, Basil Butcher, Wes Hall and Sonny Ramadhin. They wanted to be treated as equals, not subordinates. That was the heart of the argument about captaincy. Worrell (1924–1967) finally broke the barrier and his team was given a tickertape reception watched by half a million people in Melbourne at the end of one of Test cricket's all-time great series in 1960–1. Tragically his life was curtailed at the age of forty-two by leukaemia when he had so much more to give. Shortly afterwards he was given the first memorial of a sportsman at Westminster Abbey. Learie wrote a masterly obituary of him in six pages in the 1968 *Wisden* saying, 'his greatest contribution was to destroy forever the myth that a coloured cricketer was not fit to lead a team. Once appointed, he ended the cliques and rivalries between the players and islands to weld a team which in the space of five years became the champions of the world.'

A generous, kindly man, Sir Frank was one of the first who donated blood when Charlie Griffith hit Nari Contractor in the head almost fatally. Learie recalled, 'It was not generally known that he was the 13th West Indian captain and the first black cricketer to lead the side in a series, and was a superstitious man. During the 1951 tour of Australia he was bowled first ball by Geoff Noblet (1916–2006). Determined to make a fresh start in the second innings he changed every stitch of clothing, fitting himself out in completely new gear and walked to the wicket hoping that by discarding his old clothes he would change his luck. Not a bit of it! He was out for another first baller! As he came in, crestfallen, Clyde Walcott, the next batsman, said with a laugh "Why do I have to face a hat-trick every time I follow you?"

'His finest hours in England came in 1963 when he led his side to more glory at Lord's in what the critics said was the greatest of all Tests. He helped Butcher to add 110 on the Saturday and on the Monday morning West Indies collapsed. Asked if he was worried about this, one of his players said "No, he is asleep." He had this ability to drop off particularly at a time of crisis. After his death I wondered whether this had something to do with his illness which was obviously affecting him at this time, though no one knew he wasn't a fit man.

'Throughout his life Sir Frank never lost his sense of humour or his sense of dignity. Some nasty things were said and written during the 1965 tour but he was ever the diplomat. He lost no friends, made no enemies yet won more respect. He would always come up with a smile and a loud laugh. West Indians really laugh their laughs. And Sir Frank laughed louder than most of us. He was a happy man, a good man and a great man.' Those words also sum up Learie Constantine.

After his world tour Learie ran into more trouble over the sale of the two clapped-out steamers and chartering rather than buying the *City of Port of Spain*. He defended himself in an all-day sitting in the Legislative Council and later on the chartered vessel succeeded in running a regular service to and from Port of Spain to Tobago. Railways, roads and buses called for modernisation and the opposition wanted the antiquated engines and coaches scrapped in favour of building new roads. Dr Richard Beeching was busy in Britain scrapping a third of Britain's railways but Learie stood firm against copying his example. There were thousands of people working for his Department and it was a monumental job for one man to represent them.

In February 1961 he created a committee to persuade famous cricketers to return to the native heath. He told the House, 'Human nature is a copyist. Seeing Sobers, Kanhai, Hall and others will surely help produce other great cricketers.' Worrell had lived in Barbados but just before he died he returned to his birthplace, Jamaica. The decision was made to bury him back in Barbados. Unfortunately Learie's idea of having repatriated cricketing heroes had to be abandoned. Most of the heroes followed the money. He was soon becoming disenchanted about politicians and their bickering.

The fledgling federation was, like the creaking steamers, falling apart. His PNM party won another general election late in 1961 but he unsurprisingly announced he wouldn't stand for re-election. He was asked by Eric Williams to be the first High Commissioner of Trinidad in London and was relieved to return to London. Norma welcomed the decision and soon he was involved in the talks at Lancaster House to bring about independence for Trinidad. Most of the islands wanted to leave the Federation, either to remain under British tutelage or being independent. In May 1962 the federation came to an end and three months later independence was granted to Trinidad and Tobago.

One could say that Learie wasn't cut out to be a politician in a confrontational parliamentary situation. He was too nice. He tried to be a diplomat.

One of his opponents, Albert Gomes, a former Minister of Industry and Commerce, paid a tribute to him saying, 'He gave inestimable service to the PNM at a crucial time in Trinidad's history when there was a popular movement for political change. His immense popularity as a West Indian figure certainly contributed to the success of the PNM and this, in turn, inaugurated quite clearly a new period in Trinidad's development.'

THIRTEEN

FALLING FOUL OF ERIC WILLIAMS

The appointment of Learie as the first High Commissioner for Trinidad and Tobago was celebrated in the Guildhall at a lunch on June 14th, 1961 was universally applauded. It was quickly followed by his being knighted in the New Year Honours. Harold Macmillan was prime minister at the time and as a humanitarian he wanted to see the influx from the Caribbean settled peacefully after recent riots in Notting Hill in 1958, which lasted for two weeks. It started with 400 white youths termed 'Teddy Boys' attacking the houses of West Indians in Bramley Road. It spilled over to other areas and there were 140 arrests and 108 were charged with various offences including grievous bodily harm, affray and being in possession of offensive weapons. Seventy-two white and thirty-six black youths were all given five-year sentences and fined £500. The disturbances were followed by the creation of an annual Notting Hill Carnival to show the good side of West Indian culture and despite large numbers of police each year the event is still marred by drug-taking and various criminal acts, though on a lesser scale.

Learie played an unobtrusive role in the years to follow and often gave legal advice to West Indian victims and those who were unfairly treated by the police. The riots were alien to the English way of life and seeing him later becoming a 'Sir' was appreciated not only by cricket lovers but most of the population. He joined a select band along with Sir Jack Hobbs and Sir Len Hutton, all three of them genuine, decent heroes who inspired youngsters.

Almost half of his life was spent in England and if there had been a poll to find the most popular Anglo-West Indian in the United Kingdom he might have been a short favourite to come first. But his easy, friendly relationships with people of all colours and creeds soon created problems and his tenure of High Commissioner only lasted two years. A friend said of him, 'There was nothing crafty, cunning or corrupt about his politics which seem to be prevailing qualities of character to expect in many a politician today.'

In her book *A Look at Learie Constantine* Barbadian-born Undine Giuseppi wrote, 'Perhaps the political "game" is no longer a game in which a gentleman can take part and remain at the same time untainted. Learie Constantine was always the complete gentleman. Ever courteous, with an almost Victorian reverence for good manners, he sought at all times to avoid the "falsehood of extremes". It is unfortunate that he fell upon an age when "extremes" have become the normal pattern, especially where public affairs are concerned. This left very little room for the Constantines of this world to manoeuvre in, however lofty their principles. He was once asked by a fellow Minister in Trinidad how he managed to keep calm among the bedlam of the Legislature. He replied "Is not a Minister to be allowed to be a gentleman?"'

As the first High Commissioner there was no guidebook giving advice to the holder except maintaining contact with members of the British and Trinidad governments and others, the members of the Diplomatic Corps and to be concerned with the welfare of the nationals of the UK and Trinidad. He saw himself as 'a PRO of the highest status. One tries to sell one's country to the outside world. Part of the PRO function consists in going to diplomatic parties. The real burden of the job is fending for the welfare of one's own countrymen. With so many more West Indians – more than 115,000 – there now than 10 years ago the problem has been magnified.'

He went to the Thanksgiving Service in Westminster Abbey in August 1962 for the Independence celebrations of Trinidad and Tobago and three months later he was received in audience by Her Majesty the Queen. Apparently they got on very well.

His popularity was enhanced in April 1963 when the BBC invited him ostensibly to be interviewed in one of their programmes and found himself exposed to a cheering audience of relatives, friends and admirers in one of the *This is Your Life* series with a smiling Eamonn Andrews coming towards him holding a large, red book about Learie's life. Realising he had been duped, he burst into one of his mega laughs. Norma began the hour-long programme by talking about how they first met, how she once gave an ultimatum to him 'Either cricket or me!' Over the happy years of their marriage he opted for both and got away with it.

Gloria was flown in from Trinidad where she was teaching and talked about her father's difficulties in plaiting her hair when Norma wasn't available when they lived in Nelson. Asked if he was strict, she laughed and said 'Very strict!' But he was the less strict parent: Norma could be very firm. Learie's brother Elias was also flown in from Trinidad and he talked with a chuckle about the way the family used to hurl oranges or coconuts in endless fielding practices to each other and hit out with their hand-carved wooden bats. Mrs Bessie Braddock, the MP from

Liverpool Exchange, spoke jokingly about Learie's work as a welfare officer in Liverpool helping to overcome the problems of immigrants from the Caribbean well before Windrush. Former England leg-spin bowler and writer Ian Peebles described him as 'the best entertainer of the lot.' Learie didn't disagree. The singer from his birthplace, Winifred Attwell, was the next guest, admitting that when she first met him she was star-struck. Betty Snowball, one of the chief pioneers of English women's cricket, spoke of his 'wonderful coaching'.

Eric Williams was still on friendly terms, barely perhaps, and paid tribute in a filmed contribution. 'It was extravagant nostalgia,' said Learie. Millions saw the programme and his rating as a man, a cricketer and diplomat shot up.

A week later Learie received the Freedom of Nelson and he was the first person in that part of Lancashire to be given a Blue Plaque on the front wall of the house he lived in, 3, Meredith Road. Twenty or so years had elapsed since he played at Seedhill, Nelson's cramped cricket ground. Alderman John Shepherd said, 'If the title of a great man ought to be reserved for him who cannot be charged with indiscretion or a vice, who succeeded in all he undertook, and whose successes were never won at the expense of principle, justice, integrity, nor by a sacrifice of single principle, then this title will not be denied to Sir Learie Constantine.' There was loud clapping around the Council Chambers. Learie replied, less wordily, and brought more laughter when he thanked them for doing all this 'for the little dark fellow who came from a country they knew nothing about.'

Shortly afterwards he delivered a punchy lunchtime speech at the Royal Commonwealth Society. E.W. Jim Swanton introduced him saying, 'he excited and charmed and enhanced and infuriated us all on the cricket field.' In his response Learie summed up the current cricketing situation in South Africa saying, 'Black men cannot go to South Africa and that needs to change.' Of the state of West Indies captaincy – Frank Worrell had assumed the captaincy in the current tour – he said, 'This year Worrell has been appointed captain, the West Indies wisest thinker, at the edge of his retirement. But other people less talented than himself, less knowledgeable, had been selected as captain before because we had a South African attitude in the West Indies.'

He didn't say it but the thought occurred among the more enlightened of the audience that he should have been captain of the West Indies. In 1935 he took over briefly during a Test when the white captain Jackie Grant was injured. That could be considered as being big-headed but it was true. Swanton believed that Learie sometimes praised himself too much, pointing to his moderate first-class figures, but he had a lot to brag about, reaching the high notes which others didn't match, or better.

Early in May 1963 nearly all of Learie's integral work with the two races, white and black, was suddenly swamped by the Bristol Omnibus Company Affair and it forced him to quit as High Commissioner. A Jamaican had been refused a job as a conductor and he took the case to their union. A protest was staged and Learie took the side of the man and made plans to visit Bristol to help to find a solution and also to attend Gloucestershire's match against the West Indians. Another sensitive part of the story was the port of Bristol, which pioneered slavery.

One of my first meetings with Learie occurred when I was reporting on the Saturday of the West Indian match in 1963 for the *Daily Sketch* when he sat in the Gloucestershire committee room watching Charlie Griffith bowl out the home side for 60 with his deadly yorkers. Charlie's analysis of 17.3–4–23–8 was shatteringly intimidating and some observers thought his yorker, bowled at a quicker pace, should have been no-balled.

Syd Buller, England's best umpire of that era, was standing at Griffith's end and no took action. The unobtrusive David 'Smudge' Smith (1934–2003), the former Bristol City left-winger, had plagued the West Indians with his fizzy, accurate medium-pace bowling earlier in the day, rewarding him with an analysis of 17.5–9–25–5. West Indies made a mere 89. Griffith, with 22, was their top-scorer. A crowd of 7,000, crammed into its capacity, saw an extraordinary day.

Learie stayed with friends in Clifton over the weekend and stayed on to see the second day's play on the Monday. The local news reporters heard he had been there and asked him if he could speak on the row about the decision by the Omnibus Company not to employ the Jamaican. He didn't hesitate. He said, 'For it to be happening in Bristol of all places is even worse when you remember the West Indian sugar cane industry has helped, through the slaves sent from this country, to make Bristol great. The evidence is quite clear that in the Bath branch of the company coloured people are employed as bus crews and it cannot be right on ethical grounds for there to be one policy for Bath and another for Bristol.'

The Omnibus Company retaliated saying that there was no colour bar in their organisation and employers were recruited on merit. Dr Oliver Tomkins, the Bishop of Bristol, weighed in on the side of Learie at Christ Church in Swindon on the Sunday and said, 'White workers have no right to denounce racial discrimination in South Africa or the southern States in the United States and then practise it in England.' Paul Stephenson, head of the West Indies Development Council, organised a protest demonstration, poorly attended, and Learie gave an interview to the BBC and said, 'the problem might be not one of colour but of a fear by bus employees that more workers would mean less opportunities for overtime.' Griffith ensured that there was no overtime on the Monday with his figures of

15.4–2–35–5 along with Gary Sobers' 37–8–75–4, bowling out Gloucestershire for 214. West Indies won by 65 runs.

Griffith was at his peak in that match and I asked Ken Barrington, who was one of the first to say he chucked his yorker, whether he ranked in the list of the world's fastest bowlers. He replied, 'He certainly was the fastest I ever faced.'

Some weeks later Bristol Omnibus Company and the Transport and General Workers Union came to an agreement but Learie kept the argument going, writing in a Bristol newspaper: 'Do those persons who advocate reserving all their jobs for white people agree to the reasonable corollary that British people working in the coloured Commonwealth should receive the same treatment? More deplorable is the fact that this sanction is imposed because of colour only since foreigners who cannot be readily identified by the colour of their skins are always welcome.'

He intimated that the British government was putting restrictions on West Indian immigration whereas Maltese were given preference. Eric Williams wasn't happy with the way Learie handled the issue, particularly as the man in the centre was a Jamaican, not a Trinidadian. If it had been a Trinidadian there might have been the need to have his High Commissioner interfere. Relations between the two parties, Learie and Eric Williams, suddenly cooled and further deteriorated when Learie heard a rumour saying that Duncan Sandys (1908–1987), son-in-law of Winston Churchill and Secretary of State for the Commonwealth Relations between 1962–4, had lodged a complaint about Learie's alleged interference in Britain's domestic affairs. Sandys had returned from a tour to the Caribbean and may well have brought up the subject with Dr Williams' government. Learie's own inquiries failed to substantiate the rumour but concerned about his position as High Commissioner he journeyed to Port of Spain hoping to see Dr Williams. The Prime Minister declined to see him. Saddened, he returned to London and announced his resignation in February of 1964 at the end of his term. His biographer Howat said, 'He looked after his staff and was respected by other diplomats but he blundered in the Bristol affair. In the language of the game he loved… his timing was wrong though he was full of good intentions.'

That was probably the lowest point in his career. A Trinidadian writer observed, 'He was too sensitive and outspoken to steer clear of the pitfalls of diplomacy. He had been a victim of his own reputation.' In a broadcast on December 24th, 1963 Learie said, 'It was while I was recovering from an attack of bronchitis and watching the West Indies play Gloucestershire at Bristol I got dragged into the Bristol bus dispute. It had been openly stated that no coloured person would be employed either as a conductor or as a driver of a bus in the City of Bristol. I was asked to look into the trouble and quickly decided to raise the level of the negotiations because those immediately involved had adopted fixed positions and wouldn't budge. I went to the Mayor, and then returned to see Frank Cousins whom I had known well, and indeed been friends with, since working in the Ministry of Labour. I knew that his Union opposed a colour bar and I know that the Transport Board were against it too, so it was clearly a matter of asking them to enforce their own convictions. This they did. We now have coloured conductors and motormen on the buses in Bristol.'

Back at his flat in Grove End Road, not far from Lord's cricket ground, he discovered that thieves stole his Knight-Bachelor insignia and other pieces. Cricket came to his aid. Signed up as a BBC commentator on matches on Sundays, he brought freshness and humour to his new work. Nelson CC was hard up and asked him if he could play at Seedhill to raise money. On the Saturday the match was interrupted by heavy rain but the club managed to arrange a few hours of play between the showers. He was in his sixty-third year but impressed with his accurate swing bowling delivered at a much reduced pace. The match raised £127, enough to keep the bailiffs away.

Another cheering occasion was when he was elected an Honorary Bencher of the Middle Temple nine years after he was first called to the Bar, unprecedented for a junior barrister. In the citation it 'conferred on men with eminence whom the Benchers would like to dine with them from time to time.'

Just before he resigned as High Commissioner when he gave no reason to his loyal staff he spoke in a broadcast about the outcome of the Bristol Omnibus Affair: 'This is now a happy situation but unfortunately my part in bringing it about was a minor one. I got into trouble with my government. Suffice to say that among other things my government felt I had exceeded my duties and I should have recognised it as an internal matter for management and unions and refused to intervene. That may be right and I am sure that once I am rid of the protocol and conventions of the office of High Commissioner I shall be able to do a better job for my countrymen. My wife and I will certainly stay on in England.'

Three years later he was interviewed by Rex Alston in a BBC programme *Time of my Life*. Asked about the Bristol controversy he came to the point and explained the reason – 'I found myself being criticised by my government and I took the view that when a coloured man in London is getting his pants kicked the people to kick his pants don't remember he is a Jamaican or a Trinidadian or St. Lucian. It's a coloured man who's getting kicked and so for my government to take the view that because he was a Jamaican I had no right to intervene, I could not accept.' Williams never met Learie again and never spoke with him again. It was a lifelong ban but it was a short one. When Learie died in 1971 Williams recommended him posthumously for Trinidad's decoration, the Trinity Cross. As a neutral, one's impression was that Williams overreacted. A mild reprimand might have sufficed but to sever his long-time friendship with one of his country's heroic figures was mean.

After Learie resigned as High Commissioner he contacted his old friend Sir Dingle Foot, and asked if he could resume his career as a barrister. The two men first met in the early 1950s at a protest meeting against the Protectorate territories of Southern Africa to the apartheid Union of South Africa and Foot invited him to join his practice at 2, Paper Buildings in the Temple. By this time he was living in a modest flat in Kendall Court, overlooking the busy, heavily polluted Shoot-Up Hill, NW3. Kilburn underground station was close and it was an easy journey to the Temple station. Approaching sixty-three, he wasn't going to qualify for a more senior position and specialised in criminal cases and Commonwealth disputes. His health was slowly deteriorating although he made three muted appearances in charity games in Essex. In one, he smote two huge sixes and four fours in 35 made in less than ten minutes before he came to the pavilion having had a rapturous reception.

The highly cherished Wombwell Cricket Lovers Society invited him to speak and he and his friend Sir John Barbirolli, the conductor of the Halle Orchestra, were made patrons of the Society, which continues to this day. After Learie died the Society came up with a Learie Constantine Memorial Award for the Best Fielder in the annual Gillette Cup Final. The first winner in 1972, appropriately, was Clive Lloyd, then the closest fielder to a Constantine except that he couldn't match Learie's astonishing catches made behind his back.

Learie had friends everywhere and one, Denis Howell, the former Football League referee and Sports Minister in the Labour government, invited him to become a member of the fifteen-strong Sports Council in 1965. Its aim was to advise the government about raising the standard of amateur sport and physical training. In those days obesity wasn't a problem because most people had to walk more than today although with so may rail cancellations and strikes today's commuters are being forced back on to their bicycles. Howell was the chairman and he realised that Learie would make a big impression on integrating communities and spreading goodwill. It meant a considerable amount of travelling helping to set up regional Sports Councils. Providing adequate space in inner cities for artificial pitches was another concern now the councils stopped young people from kicking balls on roads and open spaces.

His interest in African affairs took him to Nigeria in 1966 acting for Amnesty International trying to seek the release of the Federal prime minister Sir Abubakar Tafewa Balewa and several other ministers who had been kidnapped by Army officers in a civil war. Learie knew some of the prominent politicians and spent six days there with limited success. One had been assassinated and another was later released unharmed. His mission brought the tragic events to the front pages of newspapers and radio and as Howat wrote, 'He had chosen a time of despair for his only visit to the Niger from which his forebears had come.'

Previously he was actively involved with the setting-up of the Race Relations Act in 1965 making it a criminal offence to stir up hatred on grounds of race or colour. In 1967 he was appointed as one of the three members of the Board under the chairmanship of Lord Mark Bonham (1922–1994), the Liberal MP for Torrington who acted as an advisor to Jo Grimond, the Liberal leader. Captured in Tunisia in 1943 and imprisoned in Italy, he walked 400 miles to British lines and was mentioned in despatches. He was related to Herbert Henry Asquith, the Earl of Oxford and Asquith (1852–1928), prime minister of Britain between 1908 and 1916, and was related to Helena Bonham Carter, the award-winning actress. The other member of the executive of the Sports Council was Bernard Langton (1914–1982), the Labour councillor and Lord Mayor of Manchester, whom Learie knew earlier in his career.

The make-up of the population of the UK was rapidly changing in 1968. Thousands of displaced Kenyans who decided to give up their British passports once Kenya was given independence from Britain had to be granted British citizenship and settle in the United Kingdom. A second Race Relations Act was brought to cover the development. The Windrush migration soon followed and Learie was busy counselling many migrants who arrived on British shores without much cash. He campaigned vigorously for making it possible to give them loans and a clause made it illegal to refuse loans but often they were turned down and left depending on friends and relatives. By this time nine more members had been added to the Race Relations Board. Learie's health had worsened but he made valiant efforts to keep up his attendance record and Howat said, 'To the end of his life he regarded his work on the Board as one of the ways in which he could be of service to a new generation of West Indian migrants.' Fifty years later the British government still hadn't resolved all the problems.

He appeared on the BBC programme *The World This Weekend* on the topic 'Should not the coloured people of the Commonwealth be given preferential treatment to aliens?' He was wholeheartedly in favour of this and criticised Conservative MPs who wanted to restrict immigration.

Another intrusion into his time came when the President of the Students at St. Andrew's University invited him to stand for the post of Rector. He visited the University on a number of occasions because Gloria was a student there and graduated as

Master of Arts and was about to go to the Institute of Education at London University. The vote on November 12th, 1967 was announced as:

Sir Learie Constantine	691
The Rt Hon. Jo Grimond, former Liberal leader	498
Alexander Gibson, conductor	281
Sean Connery, actor	178

Learie was recovering from surgery in Westminster Hospital at the time and the surprise news was greeted with joy. Grimond was a relatively popular, egalitarian politician and Sean Connery ought to have attracted more votes than 178. Four of his previous films – *You Only Live Twice*, *The Hill*, *Thunderball*, and *Goldfinger* – were box-office hits appealing to young people. Born on August 25th, 1930, at Fountainhead, Edinburgh, Thomas Sean Connery's great-grandparents came from Fife and spoke Scottish Gaelic, valid reasons for him to be favourite for the post. He had a similar poor background to Learie: his mother Euphemia 'Effie' McBain was a cleaner and his father Joe was a factory worker and lorry driver.

The new Liberal leader Jeremy Thorpe cabled Learie from Barbados inviting him to stand for the seat in Nelson. The Commonwealth Immigrants Bill had just been passed in the House of Lords on the same day and though tempted, Learie declined mainly on the grounds he would oppose the current member Sydney Silverman, a good friend of his.

Before he was installed as Rector he cabled to St. Andrew's – in those days sending a cable was almost as quick as an email – protesting against the University rugby side taking on an all-white team from the Orange Free State in South Africa saying, 'deplorable, the South African government reduces human beings to lower animals unworthy to associate with decent governments and peoples.' However, the match went ahead around the time when Peter Hain, a nineteen-year-old South African first-year engineering student at Imperial College began his campaign against the MCC (England) cricket tour to SA in 1968–9 because of the late recall to the England squad of the Cape Coloured all-rounder Basil D'Oliveira. The new South African prime minister Balthazar Johannes Vorster (1915–1983) informed MCC that D'Oliveira wouldn't be welcomed by his government and as a result not only that tour but the subsequent visit to England by South Africa in 1970 was also called off. A Rest of the World (RoW) side took over the five-match series and outplayed England 4–1 and it provided wonderful, high-class entertainment. Twelve of the twenty RoW squad was black with Gary Sobers the skipper and it included five white South Africans. In an attempt to swell the crowds the Test and County Cricket Board billed it as a Test series and the statistics were accredited to the players' Test records. Not long after their records were changed back.

Public opinion was split over the D'Oliveira affair with the Rev David Sheppard, the former England captain and later Bishop of Liverpool, heading the opposition to the tours and Gubby Allen and his supporters wanted them retained. Learie's view was: 'Speaking as a cricketer the omission of D'Oliveira is to be regretted. Speaking as a West Indian, the circumstances of the omission are positively suspicious. Speaking as a member of the Race Relations Board, even if were discrimination, it would not be unlawful under the 1966 Act, nor – as far as I can see – under the 1968 Bill.' He was one of the seventeen prominent people who signed a letter to *The Times* calling for the cancellation of the 1968–9 tour, including David Sheppard, Fr. Trevor Huddleston, Jeremy Thorpe and Sir Edward Boyle. Learie was probably tipped off by Sir Alec Douglas-Home, who was prime minister in 1963–4, eighteen months earlier saying

Vorster was always insistent that D'Oliveira wouldn't be welcome in his South Africa.

When Learie was installed as Rector of St. Andrew's University on April 17th, 1968 in the Younger Hall, one of his fellow graduands – one about to graduate – and supporters was Sir Alec who knew him previously when he was President of MCC and another one was a Scot, Sir Harold Mitchell, who was an expert in Latin-American studies with business interests in the West Indies. Learie's address to almost a thousand students was entitled 'Race in the World'. He said the honour 'had been bestowed on him in the climacteric time of his life being not far off the allotted span, there are few marks of public approbation to which I shall look back with greater pride.' His use of the word 'climacteric' might have gone over the heads of some students because it means 'reducing powers like with men losing their sexual activities.' They probably thought it meant 'climatical' – relating to change of climate.

With an audience predominantly white some others wondered why he dwelt so long on his upbringing in Trinidad and not enough on his adopted university. Despite that he was given a rousing reception. Unfortunately for him, he wasn't able to make another appearance at St. Andrew's, mainly because his health problems worsened and he wasn't fit to undertake a 1,000 miles or more rail or road trip to Fife from Kilburn and back.

Eighteen months later an unofficial meeting of students voted 151–100 calling him to resign because he wasn't able to carry out his responsibilities at the third oldest university in the world – for white students – which was founded in 1403. There have been thousands of distinguished people who have been honoured by the university but few were famous sportsmen or a different colour than white. Learie had to accept the decision and it was later ratified by the Students' Representative Council.

In the 1960s he was a TV commentator on cricket in matches for the BBC but getting up and down rickety steps to and from the cramped press boxes proved taxing. Most of the grounds didn't have workable TV and radio studios and when the John Player Sunday League started in 1969 he announced that he would no longer commentate on cricket. The BBC had invited him to serve on its General Advisory Committee in 1964 and four years later, impressed by his knowledge of the medium and his keen sense of humour, he was asked whether he would be interested in becoming a governor. Yes he was, particularly because the five-year contract brought a yearly emolument of £1,000. There were twelve governors and they met fortnightly and a car would be sent to collect him and take him back home hours later.

Another governor, Professor Glanmore Williams (1920–2005), an outstanding Welsh historian who became a firm friend of his, gave a stark reminder of his courage. 'I have seen there at times when his face was literally grey with strain and weakness, grasping for breath and wracked with bouts of the most painful coughing. Yet throughout it all he preserved the most resilient patience and good humour.'

The curse of bronchial pneumonia had gradually overtaken him and Lord Charles Hill (1904–1989), the BBC Governor General between 1967–72, an independent MP for Luton and known throughout the land as 'the Radio Doctor' said, 'Alas, the sad truth is that Learie came to us too late to play a really effective part. Already his chest had begun to give him trouble with the result that his attendance was uneven and his contribution was inevitably marred by illness. He came to us ten years late.'

Late in 1968 Learie and Norma went to Trinidad for three months to help his hay fever and bronchial problem but they realised that there was hardly improvement and returned to London. His drop in income through being not being able to work full-time as a barrister was concerning him as well. The only pension he had was the state pension and £1,000 a year from being a governor of the BBC and the same amount as a member of the Race Relations Board. He also drew expenses while working on the Sports Council.

There was a suggestion that he ought to be made a peer either in Trinidad or Britain. Opposition came from several people in Port of Spain and one of them may well have been the prime minister, the Hon. Eric Williams, who was against using British honours in a newly independent country.

Having met so many influential people and recognising Learie's unique work in bringing people together with harmony there was a growing move to make him a peer. And it soon happened when his name appeared in the New Year's Honours on January 1st, 1969. It was universally greeted not just in the UK but throughout most of the world. He chose a rather long, very grand title – Baron Constantine of Maraval in Trinidad and of Nelson in the County Palatine of Lancaster. Maraval was where he was born and brought up and Nelson where he made his name as a world-class cricketer. He said it 'must have been for what I have endeavoured to do to make it possible for people of different colour to know each other better and live well together. And it was recognition for all West Indians.'

He wasn't the first non-white peer. That honour went to the first Indian to become a member of the Viceroy's Council in India, Sir Satyendra Prasanna Sinha, KCSi, PC, KC (1863–1928) in 1919. He shared a number of remarkable coincidences with Learie. He was a barrister who completed Roman Law, like Learie, at the same Lincoln's Inn Field offices before Learie was born and worked in the WWI War Cabinet trying to bring peace and actually worked on the agreement that brought an end to the conflict. Like Learie, he made hardly any appearances in the House of Lord's because he returned to Calcutta to continue working as one of India's finest lawyers and administrators. But Learie was the first Afro-Caribbean member of the House of Lord's.

It was packed on March 20th, 1969 when he was honoured and the Earl Marshal of England, the Duke of Norfolk and the Great Chamberlain, the Marquis of Cholmondeley (1919–1990) made rare appearances to lead the procession. In third position – rather too high for Learie's batting prowess, someone mentioned – was a beaming Learie watched by a proud, beautiful Baroness Norma Constantine in the gallery above. The 16th Duke of Norfolk, Bernard Marmaduke Fitzalan-Howard (1908–1975) had his own team and as a very ordinary batsman he needed his valet umpiring at the bowler's end and when he should have been dismissed for lbw the valet would say 'His Grace is in.' Amazingly he was made manager of the England team in 1962–3 in Australia and was a big hit Down Under mainly because of his racing connections.

Fortunately Learie's hacking cough had mysteriously disappeared. Two distinguished left-wing peers flanked him, Baron Frank Beswick (1911–1987), son of a Nottingham coal miner, politician, journalist, who fought in the Spanish Civil War for the Republicans, MP for Uxbridge, an observer in the Bikini atomic bomb tests and the first person to speak in the first TV debate at the House of Lords. The second one was Baron Archibald Fenner Brockway (1888–1988), born in Calcutta, journalist, author, Labour MP for Leyton East, vegetarian, pacifist, conscientious objector who was imprisoned in WW2, a recruiting member for the Republicans in the Spanish Civil War, who included George Orwell, and a member of the Indian League fighting for independence from Britain, followed. Six months before his hundredth birthday a statue of him was unveiled in Red Lion Square, Holborn, close to where Learie was ejected from a hotel in 1943, which led to him winning the ensuing High Court action, a precursor of the Race Relations Act.

So far, despite a spirited campaign in favour of it, no statue of Learie has yet been put up in Russell Square. Camden Council, with a huge Labour percentage of members, turned down the idea saying, 'There are too many statues around Russell Square.' Where are they? Are they hidden underground? Barons Beswick and Brockway would have given them both barrels! Alongside Learie they were fervent campaigners for colonial freedom and the cause of peace.

Because of his illness Learie made only one speech in the House of Lord's on March 10th, 1971. The subject was Britain's proposed entry to the European Community. He said he would only vote for it if the seven founder countries accepted the Commonwealth Sugar Agreement to protect the Caribbean sugar industry. In Europe most countries had a surplus of sugar from sugar beet. Six weeks later the EU signed up with the Agreement. It was ironic that a grandson of a slave brought from Africa cutting cane should play a key part in saving the sugar industry in the Caribbean. Sugar is still produced there on a much smaller scale. They don't rely on selling sugar these days. Tourism has bowled it out.

On April 2nd, 1971, Learie went to Lord's for the last time to attend a lunch to celebrate Norman Preston's twenty-first year as editor of the *Wisden Almanack* and as a young cricket reporter of the Pardon's Cricket Agency, I could have been present but I was working for the *Daily Sketch* and on that day I wrote Ken Barrington's column. Ken had taken over from Learie as the big name commentator in the *Sketch*.Norman Preston's 'Notes by the Editor' about the 1971 year started on the 'Spirit of Cricket' and lambasted the Australians for their bad behaviour. He said 'they set a very bad example to young players, particularly schoolboys who like to imitate their heroes. This was the first time since 1890 Australia failed to win in a single Test in a series.' Fifty years went by and Cricket Australia – the ruling body – finally took steps to eliminate the excesses of sledging, ball tampering and 'win at all costs'. A man of high principles, Norman Preston, who lived in the Borough of Bromley, the same as me, would be delighted.

In May, Learie told his friends that he would return to Trinidad and not come back to Britain because of his health. Probably his last letter addressed to an old friend in Manchester started: 'Yes, I must go home. My health has broken down. I can stay in one place but I cannot move around without a lot of discomfort. A warm climate should help me, at least I hope so. So I am going to it. Give my best wishes of all my friends.' The letter had hardly arrived before he died on July 1st, 1971 at his home, aged sixty-nine.

FOURTEEN

EPILOGUE FOR A GOOD MAN

Like many men, good men who did much to help so many, Learie wasn't really wholly appreciated when he was alive. They are victims of the small island or country phenomena – they leave their birth place at a young age and strive to better themselves in the big city a long way away. Back at their homes where they grew up they are considered to be too big for their boots, as Learie would have said.

Trinidad Prime Minister Eric Williams who hadn't spoken to Learie since the Omnibus Company Affair, ordered a state funeral for him and the award of the Trinity Cross, Trinidad's highest honour and arranged a flight to carry his body to Piarco Airport. It was greeted by a guard of honour and a nineteen-gun salute. The lying in state took place in the Roman Cathedral Basilica of the Immaculate Conception in Port of Spain and the funeral service took place there on July 8th, 1971. There was hardly a seat unoccupied with many standing outside the Cathedral, which was started in 1816 and finished in 1851. The Archbishop of Port of Spain conducted the service and the

General Governor, Sir Solomon Hochoy, the prime minister and nearly all his ministers and diplomats from many countries and dependencies, eminent and ordinary cricketers and members of the public attended. So many that it caused a shortage of hotel accommodation in the island. A gun carriage carried the coffin through the streets lined watched by twelve-deep crowds accompanied with the Regimental Band and the Corps of Drums of the Trinidad and Tobago Regiment. There were more people than at a day's play in a Test match ground, which then held 30,000. Some schools were closed and there were a high percentage of young people.

In his speech Eric Williams described Learie as one of Trinidad's greatest sons who had earned a place in his country's history. The burial took place at the Arouca Cemetery and two months later when Norma died on September 4th, her coffin was placed next to his. Learie left his property and the sum of £3,555 which was passed on to Gloria, their family and beneficiaries. Howat's tribute was eloquently set out: 'Her devotion to her husband contributed to her own death so shortly after his, since her concern for his health made her ignore her own. When at last back at Trinidad, relations and friends realised how ill she was and there was little that could be done. She filled a key role in his life. She provided the security and encouragement he needed. She had led him to make decisions, and to regard them as his own. She had been a charming hostess and a gracious lady. Underneath her quiet, shy exterior lay a fierce determination to watch over her husband, either to prosper by his fortune or to guard his health.'

A well-attended Memorial Service took place at Westminster Abbey on July 23rd, 1971 and his friend Sir Dingle Foot gave the address. I would have gone but I was covering the second day's play between England and India at Lord's. Lord Nugent, former President of MCC and a lord-in-waiting, represented Her Majesty the Queen and Lord Jellicoe, Lord Privy Seal and Leader of the House of Lord's, represented Prime Minister Edward Heath. Eric Abbott, the Dean of Westminster, officiated and hundreds of representatives from politics, the Bar, Commonwealth, the BBC, Nelson CC, MCC and all sections of worldwide cricket filled the Abbey. Sir Dingle said, 'I have never met anyone who inspired more wide affection among all sorts and conditions of people. When Learie made his first visit in a criminal court the Judge said, "My dear Sir Learie, what an honour to have you in my court. I have never forgotten your innings at the Oval in 1939. You must stay and have a drink with me."'

John Arlott gave five pages in his obituary in the 1972 *Wisden Almanack* under the heading 'The Spontaneous Cricketer'. He said, 'Learie came upon his historic cue as a man of his age, reflecting and helping to shape it. He made his mark in the only way a poor West Indian boy of his time could do, by playing cricket of ability and character. He went on to argue the right of the coloured people with such effect as only a man who had won public affection by games-playing could have done in the Britain of that period. No man ever played cricket for a living with greater gusto.'

Sir Leonard Hutton said, 'He was always unto himself, enjoying every minute of his game and spreading joy among cricket followers wherever he played. He ran as though his feet did not touch the ground.'

There was only one Learie Nicholas Constantine.

Lady Norma
and Lord Learie

Learie and the Queen Mother

Gloria with her parents

On Eamonn Andrews' "This is Your Life" with singer Winifred Attwell

With the Duke of Norfolk

His parents Lebrun and Annais

Outside of their Nelson home in Meredith Road

Trinidad Prime Minister Eric Williams (L) and C.L.R. James the author and activist

Barbara Castle (2nd from Left) Labour Minister with friends

Leading out the Dominion XI at Lord's

Learie with Sir Don Bradman